#BossMoms

The Inspirational Guide for Mompreneurs on Building Your Empire
and Managing Your Family with No Regrets

#BossMoms

The Inspirational Guide for Mompreneurs on Building Your Empire
and Managing Your Family with No Regrets

A COLLABORATION PRESENTED BY

DELETRA HUDSON

purposely
created
PUBLISHING

#**BOSSMOMS**

Published by Purposely Created Publishing Group™

Copyright © 2018 Deletra Hudson, LLC

Printed in the United States of America

ISBN: 978-1-947054-81-3

Special discounts are available on bulk quantity purchases by book clubs, associations and special interest groups. For details email: sales@publishyourgift.com or call (888) 949-6228.

For information logon to: www.PublishYourGift.com

The book is dedicated to my coauthors and the mompreneurs who have made the decision to step out on faith and to start living your lives out loud! You are your own boss!

Table of Contents

Grateful Expressions

I thank God for giving me the vision to birth a project that will make way for personal, mental, spiritual, financial, and physical breakthroughs to occur in the lives of every reader.

To my coauthors: Thank you Brandy, Arriel, Keya, Candice, Luberta, Tonita, Kimberly, Nicole, and Affton for having faith in me to tell your story. I know this collaboration was ordained because the coauthors were not solicited, but instead handpicked and sent to me to be a part of this project. I am truly blessed to have had the opportunity to collaborate with such a wonderful group of women who trusted me and my God-given vision to empower, educate, and motivate other women to be their own bosses while being a mom.

To my children (my Legacy Keepers): Thank you Jordan, Jada, and Anthony Jr. (AJ) for being my inspiration, for encouraging and supporting me to live my dreams of owning my business and writing my books, and for loving me so much as your mom. These works and memories will be parts of my legacy that you can share with your children and generations to come. Love you infinitely!

To my family and friends: Thank you for believing in and trusting me to be great when I couldn't see the greatness within myself.

Introduction

The ability to give birth is a gift that God bestowed upon women so that they may carry on their families' legacies. The actual act of giving birth is the conclusion of nine months' worth of preparation, planning, and dreaming. As we approach the anticipated time for delivery, the birthing anxiety kicks into high gear. We start tidying up our lives, our minds, and our households in preparation for the new addition.

Being a mom is a blessing that only females get to experience. Female humans, animals, and insects alike go through preparation processes for their new offspring. We also experience the processes of cultivating and raising our offspring to be adults. These processes are all done so that lineages may be protected and legacies passed on. This book speaks about the woman's birthing process of her gifts and talents, her maternal responsibilities and instincts, and her identity as an individual.

Women are all created differently. Therefore, our birthing experiences are different. I guarantee you that no two birthing experiences are the same. The similarities that we share might be put into two categories: easy or difficult. Some of us are blessed with smooth pregnancies and easy breezy birthing, while others have difficult pregnancies with excruciatingly painful deliveries. Either way, the end reward helps us to forget about the long, tiring, and/or painful process. But over time, not only do we forget about the process and the pain, we often forget about the person and the dreams that existed before the birth.

As mothers, we wrap our big, loving, and nurturing arms around others and their dreams and goals, while putting our own dreams and goals on the back burner. I know because I did it for seventeen years of my life. How can I be so exact about the number of years? Because that was how old my oldest daughter was when I decided to step out on faith and wholeheartedly pursue my dream of becoming an entrepreneur. I did it and I loved it. After I gave birth to my dreams, I couldn't understand why someone wouldn't follow their passion and/or own their own business. It was about a year after starting my business that I realized I had to help women have a direct hand in their finances and business ventures. It was at that point in my business when I committed to bringing other moms with me on this prosperous journey.

As women, when we connect to our desire to start living our dreams and building our businesses, we find that something within us sparks and starts to grow. We find that the products, services, or visions that God has impregnated us with put us in the mindset to once again prepare for birth and the delivery of our gifts to the world. I am thankful that God armed me with information to help empower, educate, and motivate women and to give them an opportunity to deliver what has been growing within them. This process is called "Living the Dream."

The purpose of this book is to inspire, motivate, and empower moms to start or grow their business while raising their families. After I received the vision for this book, I shared my excitement and invited others to join me on this empowerment journey. Visit after visit, call after call, I continued to share my excitement about my vision and the audience was already there, awaiting its delivery! This is evident by the fact that many of the women became my clients, or women were introduced to me by those already in my circle. Many are moms who are working on or starting their own businesses and working unselfishly for others and were never able to be their own bosses. They were doing what moms do: taking care of the family and allowing their goals of business ownership to fall last on the totem pole. Like I said, I know this to be true because I was this same exact way.

As I continued to share my vision, I began to plan and prepare for the book's delivery. I knew I couldn't empower a massive number of women all by myself. So, I sought out other moms who were bosses in their own right and had turned that mentality into businesses. Many of these women are experts in their field. I asked them to share how they started their businesses while raising their families and how they learned to do both well. Nine magnificent moms answered my call and decided to trust me, and the platform I created, to share their gifts and stories.

I call these women BOSS (Business Owners Seeking Success) Moms, and they are committed to being surrogates to help you birth your dreams. These women were personally selected for you!

Each woman will tell you her Boss type and how she came to be a Boss. We first learn what it means to be a Boss and to accept abundance as your birthright. Then, the Money Boss teaches you that "you control your money; your money doesn't control you." The Customer Service Boss stresses the fact that you can't make money with poor customer service. The Mom Boss will share with you how to help your kids become entrepreneurs without losing yourself in the process. As moms and bosses, our lives tend to become chaotic, so the Khaos Boss proves that "if you want true peace and happiness, it is you that owns the key." We also have both a Purpose Boss and a Purpose-Driven Boss to guide you in the right direction to finding and living your purpose. However, none of these strategies work together if your mind is not prepared to handle the shift, so the Mindset Boss will motivate you to set your mind to overcome challenges and achieve goals. Once you establish the direction you want to pursue, the Self Boss will help you manage the people who support you and dismiss those who hinder your progress. Finally, regardless of what others think, the Creative Freedom Boss will share with you how to be comfortable with expressing yourself freely without limitations.

By reading their stories, I pray you will grasp hold of your dreams and decide, for yourself, that today is the day that you start living out loud. We hope to reach moms throughout the world who may be facing different challenges that may be keeping them stuck in their comfort zone—use our hashtag and keyword, #BOSSMOMS, which also happens to be the title of this book!

I challenge you to give life to your dreams. Today, I declare you a BOSS Mom!

Being A Boss Is Your Birthright

BRANDY BUTLER

Being a boss is your birthright. Just as I say this, I know that it's not a natural instinct for most women. So often we give away our power. We stare and admire other women business leaders as if they are some type of mystical creature or unicorn. We play polite with our desires and passions, while waiting for someone to give us approval to move forward in the marketplace. Meanwhile, God has already given us the keys to His Kingdom—He's just waiting for us to boldly step forward and open the door.

As I stand today, I'm a woman, a BOSS Mom, who is on fire for what I do. I'm an entrepreneur by heart. It's my daily task description. Each and every single day, I get the unique opportunity to wake up and work with other women and entrepreneurs to help them package their expertise, create influential brands that attract a steady stream of clients, and set up media and speaking opportunities. I've participated in national conferences, been featured on magazines and websites, and, by the time this book is published, I will be an author of four books.

Looking at me now, one would think that I was always happy, that growing a business came easily for me. But I haven't always been this lucky.

I know what it's like to feel trapped in your day-to-day. I used to dread waking up in the morning and I would press snooze several times before I would drag myself out of bed, get my kids ready for school, and begrudgingly head to work. And it wasn't even that I didn't have a good job. I had a great job.

You see, I was one of those women who looked like she had it all going on, at least from the outside looking in. I had the fancy cars, the nice home, the husband, the children, and the designer bags to boot. I had achieved what a lot of people consider success by means of getting multiple degrees and having not only a great-paying job, but a very niched down position. I had found a unique space for myself in IT quality assurance engineering. On paper, I had the ideal life, but I still felt like I was dying on the inside. I was miserable. My soul was screaming, "This is not all that the Lord has for me!"

Eventually I had to do some serious soul searching because, no matter how much I got promoted or what company I moved to, I still ended up at the same point: the point of despair, the point of no fulfillment. No matter how much I tried to close the gap by adding more activities and volunteering, I still didn't feel fulfilled. I felt like my unique talents and skill sets weren't being utilized to their fullest, like I couldn't incorporate them in my day-to-day work.

"Everything that you want is on the other side of fear."
—Unknown

I finally decided to take the journey into entrepreneurship. Of course, it didn't happen overnight. I had to invest in myself, learn new skills, and put myself out there in ways that I had never experienced before. The more I put myself out there, the scarier it was, but the results were that much greater.

Soon, I was able to get to the point that I stopped crying in my gray cubicle. Can you believe that? I literally used to sometimes cry on the job because I would get so frustrated at not knowing my next move. Can you relate to being miserable in your career? If so, stay encouraged! Your discomfort during this time is a tool for the promotion of your purpose.

Here's my advice for anyone who knows there's something more for them, but don't necessarily know how to wrap their minds around it: get creative and get nosy. Tune into yourself and identify your unique passions—some people call this USPs, or unique selling points. What are the things that come naturally to you? Throughout my journey of self-discovery, I identified behaviors, skills, and characteristics that have been present my entire life, but I hadn't ever leveraged in my vocation.

What I realized was that I loved technology, but I also loved business systems. In my corporate job, I always worked with business systems but now, in my entrepreneurial side, I help women understand those systems. The difference is that, beforehand, the business systems centered around organizations, but now I help individuals with their systems, all the while using my creative side, which was always left out in my past jobs.

As a boss mom, it's important that you take inventory of your professional skill set, as well as your personal skill set, and figure out if there is a way to blend them in your marketplace. It's vital that you identify your purpose. Some people may be able to automatically identify what their purposes are, but for others, it's going to be an ongoing journey of self-discovery.

If you know your purpose, you can begin to show up whole in your life, in your career, in your business. You see, I realized that, when I was depressed in my great-paying career, I wasn't showing up whole. I was showing up as a worker and I was showing up as a person with nice things. But I wasn't showing up as someone happy, someone fulfilled, someone performing the mission for which God put them on earth.

Now, because I understand my purpose, I'm able to show up to work and for my family much more. I'm so much happier and in tune with my family's needs because I understand my own needs. As a boss mom, it's important that you don't try to pour from an empty cup. You can't serve everyone else if you're not serving yourself. Put on your oxygen mask and serve yourself first! By doing so, you'll be able to be that much more valuable and effective in your personal and professional relationships.

Once you've identified your purpose—what makes you uniquely you—it's time to package up your expertise. I speak about this often with women I coach because entrepreneurship can seem like a scary thing. Here's something I want you to understand: if you've been on a job for years, even decades, you've made a couple hundred thousand, or in some cases, millions of dollars for that company. If you can do that for someone else's company, another organization's mission, then why wouldn't God help you do that for yourself?

At the beginning of my chapter, I said that being a boss is your birthright. Do you hear me? Being a boss is your birthright. I want you to affirm this and speak it out loud to yourself.

"Being a boss is my birthright! Being a boss is my birthright!"

This comes from the saying and universal truth, "Abundance is your birthright." When we see other boss moms and what they've been able to do in their life or their business, we often see rags to riches story. If God did it for one, He can do it for another. We live in an abundant world of infinite possibilities. Those infinite possibilities not only exist on your job, but they also exist in your business. You've got to keep that light within. Just like abundance is your birthright, being a boss is your birthright. You don't have to be a worker if you don't want to be. But let me be clear: if you want to be a worker, there's absolutely nothing wrong with that. Jobs are blessings. You can still be a boss even as a worker. You see, being a boss is an attitude. It's a state of being.

When you package up your expertise, you'll be able to create a whole new level of abundance for yourself because you'll have created a system around the way you perform your services, the way that you service others, and the way you provide value to the world. Through such a system, others may engage and gain value from your services more easily and comprehensibly. That's what I mean when I say package up your expertise.

So, how do you do this? When you package your expertise, you take your knowledge and structure it into either a product or service that you can sell in the marketplace. You see, that very same skill that you've been cultivating at your place of employment, you can package and work directly with other individuals or businesses under your company name. Even if you aren't in love with the primary role of your present job, more than likely there are key skills that you've honed, which will be extremely useful as a business owner.

Take me for instance: as I mentioned before, my background is Information Technology. I didn't particularly love computer programming, but I love technical systems that support business functions. Even more so, I love being creative and working with people, which is why I love the business that I am in now. I have been able to merge my appreciation of tech and love of people to help business owners brand and position themselves while leveraging technology.

It's important to note that packaging your expertise doesn't always have to link back to your day job. Absolutely not! If you have a hobby, a key personality trait that you are naturally good at, or a deep interest in a particular subject, you can package up that knowledge into some type of program, service, product, or book related to your passion. I've been able to package what I learned in my own journey toward becoming a boss mom and my investment in entrepreneurial training (my interests). I find that many of the women I work with typically package their expertise from a combination of life experience, work experience, and personal passions. Have you ever considered that your talents and experiences were bestowed upon you in order for to prosper from? You were divinely granted this knowledge to help others!

When your package up your expertise, not only are you marketing your business boldly and telling people what you have to offer, but you're showing up as a pro with defined skill sets and knowledge. A boss mom always shows up as a pro. Why get out in the marketplace and act like a total newbie when your business still demands the same skill set that you've been using for years? Remember: it's the same skill set, just different packaging.

Whenever you get nervous as a boss mom, particularly a new boss mom, here's an affirmation that I want you to say to yourself:

"I'm not new to this. I'm true to this!"

You know what you're doing. You're a pro at what you deliver. You may be doing it in a different marketplace or in a different way than you're accustomed to, but you know your content and your systems. Girlfriend, you are not new to this. Boss mom, you do this!

Once you've packaged up your expertise, it's very important for you to charge your worth. This is one of the things that I help women overcome in their businesses. We are each coded differently. I call this the brand money code: depending on how we were raised—different family and socioeconomic circumstances, different experiences we've been shaped by—we have certain money DNA that play out in the way that we package and price our services.

Many women wind up playing too small. I was guilty of this: when I first transitioned from corporate America to entrepreneurship, I felt sorry for everyone I charged because I thought that they too were broken down and didn't have money to spend. This partially had something to do with my personal life, because I had actually been laid off from my old job. Honestly, I never would have just quit corporate on my own, because I was a responsible adult, and my husband and I had three children. But God has a funny sense of humor! He puts us in situations that push us so that He can get the best out of us. He closes one door to open another.

I had to quickly figure out how to make my business actually work; up until then, I had been playing with it as a hobby on the side. I didn't have a systemized method to service my clients or generate sustainable income that would cover my and my family's expenses. I eventually got to a point to where I was working my tail off in my business, twelve hours or more during the day with little profit. I was a slave in my business, because I wasn't charging my worth. Soon, my husband and I were both tired, and I really thought that I was going to have to return to Corporate America. However, the Spirit told me that it was time for me to hold out just a little bit more.

I knew that I couldn't do it alone, so I decided to invest in a coach, one of the largest investments I've ever made. What I learned throughout that time, not only from my coach but from my own soul searching, was that I needed to come in to alignment with who I truly was. I had to give up the sob story about being laid off and heal my brand money code. You see, a funny thing happens when you go through something traumatic like losing your job: you think that everyone else thinks and experiences life just like you. Sometimes, we must stop shopping out of our own wallet.

I had to come to terms with the fact that I am worthy of abundance, because I am a daughter of The Most High and I trust God's promises over my life. Once I realized and believed that I was worthy of charging higher fees for the value that I bring to the table, my entire business experience changed. It's been the best thing that I've done. If you are someone who finds yourself over-serving and under-charging, I invite you to do the same! Charge your worth.

Don't get caught up in someone else's story and plan strategically. Figure out what you need to cover your minimum expenses versus how much you want to make, and then package up an equalizing price around those values. When we undercharge and over-serve, we're not only doing ourselves but also our families a disservice. Of course, we will suffer from all types of stressors and diseases resulting from them, but can you imagine the impact that will have on our families? Charging your worth helps you to live in a world where you can truly see and feel abundance by being there and supporting your family, thereby leaving an everlasting legacy.

Figure out what part of your brand money code is holding you back. Is it the nurturer in you who's trying to help and save everyone at her own expense? Is it the banker in you who's scared to invest and take risks so you can't ever experience anything new? Or is it the maverick in you who just takes all types of risks without calculating the costs? What's stopping you? That's one of the things that you need to figure out in order to honor your birthright as boss.

Once you figure our your weaknesses and hurdles, recognize them when they show up and simply be willing to let go of those old money stories. For me, I had to stop making assumptions and feeling bad about what I thought people could afford to pay me. Remember: that's not your business, because abundance is your birthright, being a boss is your birthright. The moment that you decide to charge your worth, new doors and experiences will open up and benefit you, your family, and the people you serve.

When you honor what you bring to the table and operate knowing that you are a #BossMom by birthright, you'll attract greater opportunities and relationships into your life. There is no need for you to compare yourself against anyone else. Fear, doubt, and insecurity will creep upon you, no doubt, but don't allow them to permanently reside with you.

God has a unique experience carved out just for you. That experience will only be maximized when you are willing to get creative, try new things, and take calculated risks. Provisions must be made for your vision because that is your BOSS birthright.

Exercise: Name your primary expertise or interest that would provide you the most joy working in daily as a business owner.

Money Boss

DELETRA HUDSON

In January 2016, I made a conscious decision to no longer spend my time, valuable resources, education, work experience, and knowledge on helping others create strong businesses and wealth, while my family and I struggled to live from paycheck to paycheck. People such as CEO's, mayors, and elected officials relied on me to make sure that their money was tight and that the right systems were in place to keep money flowing for the entities they controlled. No longer! I decided to step out on faith, start my own business, and make a success of it.

I grew up in St. Louis, Missouri in a household with my grandmother and my cousins. I always had an entrepreneurial spirit. I remember my cousin and me selling art to other kids in the neighborhood from my grandmother's front porch. We'd set up homemade construction-paper-hand-drawn-scribble-scrabble art projects in a vivid presentation and priced them well for our consumers (nothing cost over ten cents). We turned our art gallery into an art festival. And we were lucrative: we also sold the neighborhood kids bags of chips, candy cigarettes, Now and Laters, and pickles so they would hang out, keep us company, and draw in more customers.

Even at the young age of ten, I was conscious and fascinated about making money and owning a business. I was also a leader, but I didn't know it at the time. I created a neighborhood club where the kids on our block would hold meetings in my backyard and pay dues to be a part of the neighborhood club. I would collect all the dues money and go to Green Lee's Corner Store to buy snacks so that the club members could have something to eat while we held our meetings. Who would have known that my skills of planning meetings and events as a kid would come full circle in my adult life? As a business owner now, I plan the Prosperity Networking Event, an annual business event in St. Louis, where small business owners can connect, collaborate, learn, and pitch their businesses to others. The kids in the neighborhood used to call me "The Boss," but today, I am the Money Boss! I am the voice every entrepreneur needs to hear about managing their money and making sound financial decisions.

When I was younger, I didn't take that name of the boss as a compliment. I actually thought I was being called bossy. Thank God I never gave up that boss mentality. It is because of that confidence, leadership, and risk-taking spirit that I went on to earn my MBA in finance, acquire over twenty years of experience in the financial industry, and is on my way to becoming a successful entrepreneur, community leader, and proud mom. Believe it or not, we all have a boss buried within us. Your boss may have also shown up earlier in your childhood. Sometimes, you don't recognize it until you are much older. If you think back on the things that you loved to do or came easily to you as a child, you will probably find your passion for life.

Like I said before, my passion was my entrepreneurial spirit. If you gave me an idea or a way to make my money, I would jump on it because I was not afraid of taking the risk to learn and put money in my pocket. Of course, not every one of my ventures yielded success, but as the infamous saying goes, "failure is the best teacher." After my many previous failures and sometime half-hearted efforts, I told myself in January 2016 that, this time, I would start a successful business for my family and myself. I was going to be in control of my own professional future. I was not going to be anyone's employee unless I decided to, not because I had to. I had to make this time as an entrepreneur work, because my family and I depended on it. I was hungry for professional business success and financial freedom.

In July of 2015, I left my six-figure job as a city manager for a local municipality in the St. Louis Metropolitan area. There was a new administration coming on-board, which meant a change of the guards. Although I was disappointed about leaving the position, I was grateful that God allowed me to have the experiences, savings, investments, and good credit that allowed me to live a comfortable year, after my departure, without worrying about bills or wanting for anything. Since I didn't initially have the stress of making ends meet, I spent that time being quiet, waiting, and listening for the direction of my next life journey. I didn't rush. After six months of rest and mental restoration, it came to me what my next steps in life would be. I was going to take my professional knowledge and work experience to start my own business. But this time I was going to do it the right way, with professional help.

In January 2016, I hired a business coach. During my introductory call with her, I explained that I was a serial entrepreneur who'd never produced profitability but was ready to this time. I had to be successful on this journey because my family's survival depended on it—this business was going to be my only source of income. I needed my coach to hold me accountable to achieving and exceeded the goals that I outlined to her.

Not only did this woman hold me accountable to the goals I set, but she also helped me set and achieve more goals than I could've ever conceived. She motivated me to publish a book and launch a major event and book signing within three months of working with her. Today, I have sold over two thousand copies of my first children's book, *Money Doesn't Grow On Trees*.

My business coach was one of the best investments I made in myself, personally and for my business. Brandy Butler, my amazing coach, is also a coauthor in this #Boss-Moms collaboration, sharing her own boss story.

As moms, we make many sacrifices and put a lot of people and their welfare ahead of our own. But on my journey to become the Money Boss, I worked hard to achieve my own personal goals. There was a time in my young professional life when my credit was bad, I had to file for bankruptcy, and I lived from paycheck to paycheck. I didn't live this way because I didn't have money—I lived this way simply because I didn't know any better.

I grew up in a household where we didn't talk about money. Money conversations were for the adults and kids. We were trained to stay out of grown folks' business. Needless to say, when I went away to college, I took every credit card they offered and maxed it out on my needs and wants. Unfortunately, my family didn't know any better. I was the first in my family to go away to a four-year college, and we were all financially illiterate. We didn't know what we didn't know. As a result, I acquired bad credit and messy money management skills. Thankfully, after the financial hole was dug, I gained enough from my educational background to know that there were better options out there for me. However, I was not going to learn what I needed to know from a school. I was going to have to teach myself about actually applying those other options.

According to the report released in 2017 by the Financial Industry Regulatory Authority (FINRA), America is a capitalist society with a financial literacy rate of 37 percent among adults. Despite being a consumer nation, we are one of the most financially illiterate countries in the world. Why? Because the American educational system doesn't not prepare us to be financial literate, not even at the post-secondary level. Our college degrees teach us how to be an employee, not an entrepreneur. Therefore, I knew enough to know that I needed to invest in myself to learn better personal money management, but I didn't know how.

I first began by studying people who had money and mimicked their strategies. I also used my work experience in managing other people's money and started applying those strategies to my personal finances and money habits. Eventually, I transformed my financial position and my credit. I started to live the life I desired. I had achieved my definition of financial freedom by the age of twenty-four. I had a career, a house, and time and money to travel.

Twenty years later, I am now taking my entrepreneurial faith walk. I own my own financial coaching and consulting firm. I am also an author, speaker, wife, and mother of three beautiful children, who I call my "Legacy Keepers." I now empower others by paying forward the knowledge and information I gained over the years, to improve their financial position, increase their financial knowledge, and achieve the lives they desire.

Over the past couple of years, I have helped several clients take their faith walk to entrepreneurship simply by transforming their mindsets from being broke and broken to blessed and prosperous. I helped them adjust their mindsets and become conscious of their relationships with money and how it flows to them. Many of these ladies went on to leave their full-time jobs to begin their entrepreneur journeys, all within a year of our working together, and they haven't looked back. Let me help you achieve your dreams!

Here are three key principles to help you grow into becoming your own Money Boss:

Money Principle #1: You control your money.

After starting my financial coaching business, I met many women who were not aware of the fact that they were relinquishing financial control to their children, significant others, clients, and customers. Yes, clients and customers. How do I know? Because I was one such woman.

My business coach often told me that I was giving away too many of my services because I was grossly undervaluing myself. It was difficult for me to gather up the nerve to quote a higher price and hold firm to it without caving in with a lower price product just to get the sale. It really boiled down to me not having the confidence in my skills to know that I had a valuable product people needed. That product was me! It wasn't until I got comfortable with pitching my consulting services that I gained the confidence to start charging my worth without remorse.

So what was it about pitching my consulting services that gave me confidence? My consulting services consist of me sharing my twenty-plus-years of work experience and educational knowledge from the financial industry.

I create budgets, analyze financial reports, create policies and procedures to improve financial and organizational management, all while creating multiple streams of income for my clients with grace and ease. My specialized and professional consulting services make me the boss of money management. But the important thing is, my skills are my passion, which I happened to turn into a paycheck. If you are looking to start a business, create an additional source of income, and provide a service that you are passionate about and know well, convince people that you can perform the service better than anyone else. You have a special niche that others are not providing and can't match.

When I started my business, I couldn't understand why people had businesses that catered primarily to women. After a year into my coaching business, I realized that many women aren't controlling their own financial destiny and couldn't figure out how to gain that control. They were putting themselves on the back burner while they continued to provide for others. Financial advisor Suze Orman says, "When it comes to women and finance sometimes there's a disconnect between what women know and how they act, their ability as achiever and their financial underachieving, and between the power they have within reach and the powerlessness that rules their actions."

Meanwhile, Prudential Research Study shows that women are typically the decision-makers in the household, which include decisions regarding financial matters and planning. But for some strange reason, women often do not recognize the power they have. We know how to take five loaves of bread and feed thousands. We know how to take $1,000 a month to keep a roof over our six kids' heads, food in their bellies, and clothes on their backs. It isn't always easy, but we find the power and strength to get it done. So why shouldn't we transfer that mindset to our own goals and dreams? You can make it happen for yourself!

Let's not forget that many of us are making just as much, if not more money than our male counterparts. Now let me clarify, women, particularly black women, are paid less than $.70 on the dollar compared to men. However, women bring income into households that cannot be ignored. In fact, many households wouldn't survive without the income of the woman. As such, we must learn to be in control of our own financial position and destinies. Oprah Winfrey says you should be able to count your own money. I would add that you should not sit back and let other people count your money for you, even if they are managing it; this includes your significant other. Always know how much money you have!

As mothers, wives, grandmothers, aunties, daughters, and sisters, we must proclaim that we control our money and our money does not control us. We determine our financial freedom, and as the chief decision-makers for our families, it is our responsibility to pass that knowledge and mindset on to our generations to come. We must teach our children how to be fiscally responsible, set goals, and implement the plans to achieve those goals.

Money Principle #2: Teach your children good money habits.

Our children are our legacy keepers. They will take our information and habits, then pass them on for generations to come. If you desire to have more and make an impact on how future generations will have better and do better, start teaching good money habits to your children.

I previously mentioned my children's book, *Money Doesn't Grow on Trees*. It was inspired by my children and the process I used to help them understand how to earn, keep, and grow their money—what I now call the EKG of money—and the importance of good money management. Why did I write a children's book instead of a guide for adults? The reason is simple: children are the foundation of our community. In order to transform communities, we must teach the children, who will take it back to their families and help grow more intelligent communities. My goal is to educate, motivate, and empower people whether they are business owners, employees, adults, or children. The financial literacy in our country must increase in all areas of society for people to achieve the financial freedom that they desire.

Moms, I challenge you to get your children involved and raise their money consciousness. Involve them in day-to-day activities such as paying bills, grocery shopping, taking care of your house, and putting gas in your car. Help them understand what your paycheck looks like and show them how to make decisions based on needs versus wants, so that, when the time comes for them to make their own financial decisions, they will do so without intimidation.

I encourage you to start having money conversations with the children in your life. Use my book and other resources as tools. Help them decide how they can create ways to make money around the house, in the neighborhood, or through their own business, and foster their EKG of money!

Money Principle #3: Money has a specific use.

As the chief administrator of the household funds, moms understand the importance of having money in hand, because we use it to take care of our families' specific needs. You must apply this same hustle mentality to planning and growing your business. Money has a specific use. Have you ever gotten a hold of some extra money and didn't have a clear intention of what you were going to use that money for? After a while, the money is gone and you can't remember what you spent it on. The problem is that you did not use that money for a specific purpose.

Money and prosperity are God-given gifts that flow to us in exchange for doing good and providing services to others. We must be good stewards over those blessings. I challenge you to evaluate your relationship with money and determine if you have a clear purpose for every penny that comes to you. Think about that the next time you're in a position where you think you have a windfall of cash, unexpected or expected. For example, you get a tax refund. Many of us typically take that money and spend it on whatever we want or have desired or dreamed about. In fact, can you remember what you did with your last return? Did you spend it on a need or a want? If your answer is inconclusive because you can't remember, you've proven my point. Understanding your relationship with money and being conscious about the purposes you have for your money will help you acquire more and achieve your financial goals. You earn your status as a "Money Boss" and control your money when it flows to you.

Warren Buffett said, "The best investment you can make is the investment in yourself." Start living your life fully and die empty. Commit to living your dreams out loud and creating a legacy that you pay forward to future generations. Find the things that you love to do and start making money from them. What will you do today to get on the road to being a Money Boss?

As the boss, we assume responsibility for our successes and failures. There is no difference when it comes to being the Money Boss. As the Money Boss, you assume full responsibility over the financial position of your life, family, and business. As William Ernest Henley says his poem "Invictus," "I am the master of my fate; the captain of my soul."

You control your destiny and yourself. Do it with pride, and know that others are watching, especially your Legacy Keepers!

Mom Boss

ARRIEL BIVENS-BIGGS

I'm what you might call a Mom Boss. I've always been an entrepreneur, inspired by my mother and grandmothers, all strong, big-hearted women who were proactive in the lives of their children and communities. One of my favorite scriptures is Proverbs 22:6: "Train up a child in the way he should go: and when he is old, he will not depart from it." I am the person I am today because of their unwavering love and support. Like them I plan to leave a legacy that says, "If you can envision it, you can make it count."

There are three major things I would like you to take away from this chapter on your journey to becoming a Mom Boss:

1. Read books that will help you grow. What you put into your mind is what will come out. If you are putting positive things into your mind, the more positive you will become.

2. Watch the company you keep around your children. If you hang out with people who talk badly and negatively to their children; you most likely you will do the same. But, if you are around people

who speak positively into their children and want them to be successful, you will want the same for your own.

3. Teach children that entrepreneurship is an option. Be intentional about teaching and communicating with your children. Love and support them unconditionally, regardless of what they choose for their lives. Let them feel free to be who they are and allow them to dream big with no limits.

I consciously and whole-heartedly declare that I am a child of God. I am also a wife to my husband and a mother to two beautiful children, Mikey and AJ. Now that I look back on my life, I've always been a Mom Boss, but I didn't recognize it until recently. It all started three years ago, when my son Mikey wanted to open a lemonade stand at the ripe age of six-years-old. Mikey asked my husband and I several times if he could open the stand, but he also wanted to play basketball, karate, golf, and a few other things. As a parent, we all know that being six means discovering new things and Mikey was open to something new and different everyday the sun would rise. Little did we know, he was already destined to become an entrepreneur.

At that time in my life, I worked a full-time job while building my photography business. I would let Mikey go on shoots with me as my assistant, helping with small things. What I didn't realize was that, all along, Mikey was learning about how businesses work. I remember sitting down to start my edits after finishing one shoot, and Mikey showed me the pictures that he had taken which looked better than what I had taken. "It's the angle, Mom," he said. I would laugh because he was 100% correct. I began paying attention and noticed he was capable of following directives like moving more quickly so that I wouldn't miss the shot.

One day, when Mikey was eight, he asked to get something out of the vending machine. I asked him if he knew that the money people put into the machine goes to the person that owns the machine. A light bulb went off in Mikey's head and he decided in that moment that he wanted to own a vending machine. Over time, I watched his entrepreneurial excitement grow, which made me do research to support him. I ran across a book called *Think and Grow Rich*. While I read it, I began taking on a new prospective. I looked up programs on entrepreneurship that would help him develop and learn.

Unfortunately, I ran into a problem: I couldn't find a program that catered to Mikey's age group and offered hands-on experience. So, I personally started teaching him about the basics of running a business and, most importantly, the mindset and traits of an entrepreneur. I was surprised how quickly he caught on. He asked more and more questions about owning his own business, specifically, owning a vending machine. I finally told him yes, but that he needed to get his feet wet with the lemonade stand, which was a more cost-friendly option at the time.

Mikey asked a friend to become his business partner. As a mom and business owner myself, I wanted them to get a realistic experience. Their business meetings started out with talking about their business, coming up with a name, deciding on a theme for uniforms, and developing a pitch. They had to decide how to market their business.

The boys first had to learn about investors and sponsors. During one of their business meetings, we went to shop for products for the lemonade stand. We stopped at a well-known party store and asked for the manager. The boys' pitch was put to the test. Afterwards, the store manager let the boys know that they had done an awesome job and that he could not sponsor money, but he could sponsor products. We went through the store, picking out things that we needed for the stand, and on top of that, the manager said that they could open the stand in front of the store. We were excited—well, mostly, I was! I didn't expect to get a prime location like that one.

When we were back inside the car, we discussed the importance of supporting people who support you. Originally, we were scouting out locations that were not in our community, but when the store manager suggested that we operate at the local store, we realized the importance of giving back to the community. We brainstormed to see what organization they could donate to and make the most impact. We started searching online and found that one of my friends from high school owned a nonprofit. I explained to Mikey that she was the lady who helped me and him through a challenge he had a month prior: Mikey's favorite words at seven-years-old were "I want" and "Can I have." I must say that I was guilty of always giving him what he asked for. Before my husband and I got married, it was just me and Mikey. I spent a lot of money on him to prove to myself that I was a good mom. I brought him things that I couldn't really afford. I worked a lot of overtime to get him the things that I never had. I would tell my husband I just wanted the kids to have a good life, but that idea of a good life was something I made up in my mind. I noticed with Mikey that, whatever he was given, he would be excited about for a few days, maybe a week. Then, he would be on to the next new thing that he just had to have.

One afternoon, Mikey asked me for a new video game and I told him, "No" He told me all the reasons why he thought he should have this game. My answer was still, "No." A little while later, he went over to his friend's house. About ten minutes went by and I got a call from Mikey's friend's mom. Immediately, she asked me not to get upset. She told me that Mikey was upset and said he wanted to stay with her. I initial got angry but had to quickly calm down.

I remembered that a friend of mine from high school often made videos on Facebook about the importance of processing what our babies are saying to us. I reached out to her (crying, of course) and she walked me through how to help Mikey express how he feels. I sat with Mikey and listened to what he was really saying to me. He told me he was accustomed to getting what he wanted whenever he wanted it, and he didn't understand how to process hearing "No" from me. In his young mind, Mommy had all the money and was saying "No" just to be mean to me. What he didn't understand was that Mommy didn't have any money and was living paycheck to paycheck. That was when I truly solidified in my mind that I was going to teach him about finance so he can understand how to earn money and buy the things he likes for himself.

Now, back to the lemonade stand: The boys loved the idea of giving to my friend's organization and called to set an appointment to meet with her. It was fun preparing the boys for the meeting, after which they took pictures like young business professionals.

The next task was to find sponsorship from family and friends. Mikey and his business partner went to work, reaching out to get money for supplies. We were fortunate to have a contractor donate supplies and his time to build the boys a stand. They even got a local small business to design their flyers. But they needed a little more cash to reach their goals, so they decided to take a twenty-dollar loan out from me that they'd pay back with 5% interest.

The big opening day was fasting-approaching, and Mikey and his partner were ready get the final supplies. As a Mom Boss, I quickly identified a teaching moment and took advantage of it by going to different stores to compare prices for all the items needed for the stand. To make the stand appealing, Mikey and his partner made the stand

Lego-themed (the new Lego movie had just come out): the napkin holders and the cash register were made of Legos. To top it off, they named the lemonade stand, Everything Is Awesome Lemonade.

When we pulled up to the store on the opening day of the event, there was a line of people, waiting to get a popular brand shoe that came out that day. So, I got the boys together and told them to go let the people in the line know what they had to offer. The boys grabbed their signs and started to sell. They worked hard that day and, at one point, people actually lined up to try Everything Is Awesome Lemonade. When they got a sip, they said, "This is Awesome!" The boys did amazing in sales.

Afterwards, I asked Mikey what he was going to do with his half of the money and he said, "Buy my vending machines." So, Mikey's Munchies was born. Today, Mikey owns and operates five machines. He takes inventory of his products, shops for supplies, restocks machines twice a month, and counts and deposits earnings into his business bank account. He then budgets $50 a month from his earnings, which allows him to pay his cell phone bills and Xbox Live subscription on time. My role as his Momager is to make sure I keep him learning and growing as I partner with him to direct his knowledge and research in the right direction. Oh, and I'm also his secretary. If you ask Mikey, I work for him: I make sure that Mikey's schedule is properly maintained and his experience is kept as realistic as possible, but timing things appropriately so that he can take the time to learn and absorb.

We soon started to talk about writing a book. My husband and I brainstormed with Mikey and helped him to write down what he learned from running his own business. During this process, we knew Mikey would need an illustrator to add the picture design to the book. The illustrator we chose referred us to a creative writing specialist for Mikey. She offered a customized online class to help Mikey with the writing process. It was extremely cool, because we worked at our own pace, filling out fourteen worksheets to use as guides to writing the book. Each time he would finish a work sheet, I could see the story coming together. From this creative writing process, Mikey wrote his first children's book called *Mikey Learns About Business*.

The book is about a nine-year-old boy named Mikey who wants to start a business, but doesn't know how. But he meets a magical briefcase named "Biz" who guides him through what it takes to start a business. Mikey learns how to write a business plan, implement marketing strategies, network, and much more. The book helps other children learn about like Mikey had.

While working with Mikey, I founded Young Biz Kidz (YBK), a 501c3 nonprofit organization that displays positive, diverse, and creative ways to teach economics and to introduce parents to a safe environment where children can learn about entrepreneurship. Our purpose is to empower youth through financial education, while encouraging entrepreneurship and developing leaders within their community. Our mission is to equip young kids with the skills and knowledge to live productive lives. Character-building, accountability, money management, work ethic, and professionalism are all core components of YBK.

Today, Mikey, the Kid Who Knows the Biz, is a ten-year-old kid entrepreneur, keynote speaker, and Amazon bestselling author. We sold over a thousand copies of his book in six months. He has been featured on local news stations and was a part of the National Urban League Conference 2017, and travels to other states to tell other youth about his experience. As a member of YBK, he is a leader in his community by helping to teach financial education, leadership, and entrepreneurship skills to his peers. He is now investing into his college fund and in brands that he used to spend money on, such as Nike, Jordan, Apple, etc.

Doing all of this with children and my own son often reminded me of how I started out in business. In elementary school, I sold candy. In middle school, I added bead jewelry to my inventory, and in high school and college, I braided hair. Here's my definition of an entrepreneur: a person who is creative, innovative, and able to solve problems. See, for me, entrepreneurship was something that already existed in me and was a part of my uniqueness. When I first started creating bead jewelry for myself and braiding my own hair, it was because I didn't have the money to pay someone else. Soon, people started to seek me out for services that I was offering only to myself. My friends and family would call me and ask me how much I charged for my services, and I just gave them amount off the top of my head without considering the amount of time that went into whatever product/service I was working on at time. This came from my lack of knowledge about business. Honestly, at the time, I was just excited about having the ability to make my own money on my own time.

I attended college in Iowa and, to keep from getting a part-time job, I braided hair. There weren't many braiders in that area so I was in high demand. I started braiding for my school's men's basketball team, and after games, the players from the other teams would ask about their braider. At times, I braided up to eleven guys' hair in an evening. The cool part was, because I was the only braider they knew, I could charge what I wanted. I charged twenty dollars per guy and I could pick the style I wanted for them.

When I came home from college, I got a job. That's why you go to school, right? Now, I enjoyed college, but what I went to school for was not what I was passionate about. If I could go back in time, I would say to my younger self, "Follow your passion because your passion will lead you into your purpose." As testament, the joy I get today from working with youth is unexplainable. The pride I feel when seeing them succeed is unattainable in any other way. Getting to hear all the amazing ideas is priceless.

YBK has opened our youth up to creating business opportunities that they design themselves, whether they are creating custom bracelets, wallets, headbands, keychains, or baked goods. The YBK experience includes being exposed to radio interviews and videos, learning effective communication, building self-esteem, budgeting and money management, learning the importance of credit, and building strong relationships. It's really cool to see parents and children get excited about their small businesses. Beyond that, YBK and God have opened doors for me that I never thought was possible. Growing up, I watched my mom work with youth as a director of a community center, and now that I'm older and in this role, I understand why my mom enjoyed the flexibility of her job. She could bring her kids to work while helping other youth in the process. To this day, she still communicates with many of the children who passed through the community center.

I now have the freedom to be me, all while spending the day at Chuck-e-Cheese, eating ice cream and French fries, having a pillow fight in the middle of the day, volunteering at school, scheduling a meeting, closing a deal, or creating an event. I can now see myself as a part of the solution, creating new and different ways to teach financial education while helping to raise the next generation of successful business owners and community leaders. I'm also now a parent engagement specialist who uses the tools of entrepreneurship to reach the masses. My desire for YBK is to have centers nationally and to be known as the place where parents can take their children to develop entrepreneurial skills.

My hopes as a Mom Boss are to encourage the next mom to listen to and strategize with their children. Their big dreams need encouraging. I spend a good deal of time listening to Mikey. Because he knows I'm listening to what he says and his new ideas. He keeps his phone in his pocket at the dinner table! It also helps that we're his number one investors.

Making sure that your children are prepared for the real world and are introduced to the life experiences money offers, when used appropriately. Make sure to identify and take time to indulge in teachable moments, always letting your children know that entrepreneurship will be an option for them. If they decide that college is not for them, that's all good, so long as they feel confident in creating steady incomes for themselves and their families through the power of entrepreneurship.

In our household we build legacies. The importance of financial literacy, entrepreneurial mindset, and leadership are key qualities needed to live a productive life and to be passed on to future generations.

Customer Service Boss

KIMBERLY D.L. PITTMAN

I love the television reality show, Shark Tank. Entrepreneurs are allowed the opportunity to present their ideas and/or products to a panel of multi-millionaires in the hopes of obtaining their financial backing and mentorship. I have watched every episode since the series premier in 2009. Subsequently, I've ordered many products that have aired on the program. For the most part, I've been pleased with everything that I've patronized from the show. However, I recently had a bad customer service experience with one of the featured businesses. It was disappointing considering they presented a promising product and I was truly excited to support them.

Unfortunately, this happens way too often with companies and their entrepreneurs. There is often a great idea and a brilliant business plan on how to execute the marketing and finances, but very little thought put into customer service and maintaining a high level of professionalism at all times.

Well, guess what, Boss Mom? Each and every time you meet someone, they are a potential customer. In a sense, every meeting, every call is your very own Shark Tank.

Each sale you make, no matter how small, is an investment in your business. Are you prepared to provide a quality of service that will complement the quality of your product?

"Customers may forget what you said but they'll never forget how you made them feel."

—Unknown

When I ask a group friends whether or not they would use a locally owned shop or service, the majority reply that they'd prefer to use a "known" brand. I ask why that is and they say that past experiences with poor customer service, lack of professionalism, and failure to meet deadlines deter them from choosing a mom-and-pop shop over a known conglomerate. Personally, I prefer to use locally owned shopping and service venues, but I can relate to my peers. Unfortunately, the few bad apples of small businesses have earned the entire orchard a bad rep.

This is why I started my first business, KDLP Enterprises, back in 2002. KDLP Enterprises is a small business-consulting firm that encourages and coaches novice business owners and entrepreneurs on the rules of corporate business etiquette. At the time that I founded KDLP, I was working full-time in the corporate world of healthcare administration. I worked my way up from entry level to management in a matter of four years and continued to work within the medical and dental revenue cycle for a total of twenty-two years, all while running my consulting business on the side.

My goal as a consultant is to help business owners polish their appeal to the public. I teach the importance of professionalism in all aspects of the business from the logo to the website, all the way to invoices that go out of the door. I always stress that a polished outward appearance combined with the feel of the neighbor-next-door customer service is what gives the local entrepreneur a leg up on the commercial competition. In my years of working side by side with many local BOSS Moms (and Pops), I have learned that it is not a lack of commitment to their business, but a lack of time and proper budgeting that keeps many from retaining the clients that they worked so hard to procure. An unreturned phone call, an unchecked email, an unanswered social media inbox message are all more than just traffic statistics that prove how well your marketing is performing. It all translates into lost revenue.

Nobody likes to see money walk away, yet that is the result of poor customer service. In this chapter, I'm not going to tell you how to run your business or sell your product, but I will introduce you to the ACE method and help uncover the bare necessities needed to lay the foundation to strong, long-lasting, successful customer service that will allow you to retain your business relationships that you worked so very hard to secure

"People expect good service but few are willing to give it."

—**Robert Gately**

You have a fantastic product. We already know this. If you did not have a fantastic product, then you would not be secure enough in yourself to take the leap to become a Boss Mom. My question for you is this: if you were awarded the opportunity to be on Shark Tank right now, would you be able to handle the influx of business inquiries that this marketing magnet produces? Let's re-visit my bad experience that I briefly mentioned in the beginning.

While watching the infamous entrepreneurial funding show, I immediately went to one entrepreneur's website on which they were selling dolls. I don't have any young daughters of my own, but I made it my business to find something that I could order. I ordered a tee shirt and an affirmation book for my ten-year-old goddaughter. It wasn't a large purchase, only a total of $38.79, but it was my small way to show support to a blooming brand.

The website was lovely. The products were as presented on the Shark Tank episode and everything seemed reasonably priced. The order went through without a hitch. The money was deducted from my account and I received my electronic receipt. The following day, I received an automated "Thank You" message along with my order number and a note that a tracking number would be sent shortly after. Two weeks passed and my goddaughter never received anything. I checked my emails and I hadn't received any other follow-up messages. I double-checked my PayPal account to make sure that the payment went through without any mistakes. Once I verified that everything was clear on my end, I decided to give them a little more time. I understand how overwhelming running a business can be. My patience paid off because a few days later, I received another blast email from the company.

They explained that the doll orders had been delayed due to the production partners taking a "longer than expected holiday observance for Chinese New Year" and that we could expect the dolls to ship in early March. While I appreciated the email notification, this did not necessarily pertain to me or the order that I'd placed. The following week, I made several attempts to call the company with the phone number provided in the blast. When I finally got through and spoke to a live operator, I was given the standard "I will have someone look into it and give you a call back." I was happy with that response. I realize that things happen and it takes time to research shipping mishaps.

Another two weeks pass and there is no phone call, no email, no anything. No one is answering the phone. No one is returning my email inquiries. At this points, six weeks had passed since I placed my order. What is an ignored customer to do? Social media, of course! I check the Facebook page, only to discover that I am not alone. There were many, many complaints from others who were also waiting on orders. Some of them had placed orders months ago. The company had a recent post thanking everyone for their support and continued patience and asking them to continue checking their emails for the blast notification concerning the shipping delay. I responded very respectfully asking for status on orders that did not involve an actual doll. I left my order number in the comments for easy access and, to my relief, the page administrator responded to my inquiry.

> The email only covers information regarding the shipment of dolls. An earlier post stated non-doll items would be mailed last Monday. Has this been changed as well? Order #2368
>
> Like · Reply · February 4 at 5:43pm
>
> Hi Kimberly! Your order should have shipped last week. Checking on it now, will have an update for you by tomorrow morning. Unlike · Reply · 1 · February 5 at 10:15am

Unfortunately, I did not hear from the company. I waited another month before reaching out to them again. This time I decided to use instant messaging on Facebook since they appeared to be active on the page, posting ads and asking people to place orders, even though current customers were threatening to contact the Better Business Bureau for lack of customer service.

MAR 9TH, 7:29PM

Hello, I just need to know the status of order 2368. Just a tee and a book. That's it. No doll. Order placed back on Jan 7th. I realize you have your hands full and I don't mind being patient, however I'm not getting ANY communication regarding NON-DOLL orders. Thank you so much. I love the idea, but please ...please ..PLEASE... improve on your customer service. Too many of us are feeling ignored. If you need help responding, I would even help with that VOLUNTARILY. I believe in you just that much! But the non-communication is a definite way to lose trust. Much love and PLEASE respond so I can let my god-daughter know something.

I was greeted with the automated response:

"Thanks for messaging us. We try to be as responsive as possible. We'll get back to you soon."

Three weeks passed and still no response directly to my inquiry. There have been two additional email blasts and a Facebook live post with explanations for unexpected shipping delays and more plugs to buy new merchandise.

I am not angry about not receiving the goods; I am disappointed in the way the situation was handled. However, with every situation there is a silver lining and this experience has become my latest case study. We will use this example to exemplify how this company could have integrated excellent customer service skills that would've kept their clients loyal.

"Customer service is the new marketing."
                    —Derek Sivers, Founder of CD Baby

The good news is, the company from this scenario did not do everything wrong. In fact, there are many things that they did absolutely correctly in maintaining basic customer service. Here is what the doll company did right:

Appearance: The company appearance is the very first thing all potential clients will see, whether it be your logo, your website, your business card, or you! Many people don't realize that excellent customer service starts with your company's image, long before one of your representatives speaks a word. One thing this company had was the appearance of professionalism. The website was easy to use and engaging. The checkout and ordering process was user-friendly.

Make sure that any images of your business that the public sees is clear, easy to read, and engaging. This includes your logo and business card—speaking of, you should always keep a business card on you at all times. It doesn't necessarily have to be an actual card, but there should be some sort of hand-out item that contains your contact information. Whether it is an engraved ink pen or a bookmark, always be prepared to give a potential customer a tangible way to get in touch with you.

Immediate responses: Another thing that the doll company did right was that they set up all of their accounts to give an immediate response to customer inquiries. When I placed an order, there was an immediate "Thank you for your order" automated response. When I voiced my concerns on the social media page, there was a fast response stating that the inquiry would be researched. When the instant message was sent, the company's automated response programming kicked in again. This may not seem like much, but automated replies are essential for all parties in the transaction. It assures the customer that their message has been received and it allows you time to respond at your convenience.

Use of email blasts: Kudos to the doll company for the many email blasts providing updates on the shipping delays. If your company ever encounters any type of glitch, blast emails are a great way to keep all clients in the loop about what is going on.

Use of Social Media- Social media can be your best friend, when used correctly. The doll company used social media to its advantage. Reiterating the information from the blast emails for those who do not check or read their emails was a brave move, as was conducting a live session to engage with their many angry customers.

"Don't find fault. Find a remedy."

—Henry Ford, Founder
Ford Motor Company

Now let's dig a little deeper to see exactly what the doll company could've done differently to help cut down the number of complaints. Take a moment to think about this: from start to finish, what's the one thing that was missing in the business to client interaction?

Communication

Yes, there were immediate responses. Yes, there were email blasts giving updates. Yes, there were social media postings. How much more communication could have been done? A lot more! Is there such a thing as too much communication? Absolutely...and never!

That may sound conflicting, but the truth of the matter is both answers are correct. If you are pushing to make a sale, some clients can be turned off with the constant requests to "Buy! Buy! Buy!" Be sure to gauge your clients and know when to back off so as not to offend potential supporters. However, if there is a problem with the delivery of a paid product or service that will cause missed deadlines, there can never be enough communication. Money is a sensitive subject. Everyone works hard for their cash and the fact that they choose to spend it on your company means that they trust you to deliver and that, in turn, you will value and respect them. Lack of communication translates into a lack of respect. We never, ever want to disrespect our customers and clients. They are the reason that we do what we do and are able to pay our bills.

How could the doll company have handled things differently? Well, for starters, they could have been honest about their inventory. The website, while it was beautifully constructed, was misleading. The out-of-stock products should have been labeled as such. There also should have been a disclaimer stating that all items were currently on a shipping delay with the true estimated delivery date. Personally, I don't care if the items are on a six-month delay; however, that is information that should be shared prior to entering your credit card number and not after an order is processed. I like to follow Michael Baisden's motto: "Always giving people a choice based on truth." Give the details as much as you can upfront and allow the client to make a decision. Even if you lose the sale at that time, have faith in your product or service to know that the client will return because you have forged an initial impression of trust.

Additional communication is necessary when a client reaches out to you. Your company should always, always respond personally to each and every inquiry from both your paid and potential customers. The doll company's business owners may say, "But I just sent out an email blast yesterday. It's not my fault if the customer didn't read it..." True. It may not be your fault. It may even be cumbersome to take the time to do this, but if a client has taken time out of his or her day to reach out to you, then you must value their time and ease any concerns they may have.

If you are a one-woman show who has suddenly been inundated with an influx of inquiries, solicit help from your kids to complete other tasks. While you cook dinner, your age-appropriate child can read the messages to you and you can dictate the responses for them to type and send. If you don't have a teenager or cannot afford to hire an assistant, check into the local business training institutes and be added to their list as an internship location. You can also check with your local church, community, and school leaders for leads on mentorship programs that will allow you to provide business training to an eager youth, who may learn from completing administrative duties for you. Regardless of what resources you use, the key point here is always respond to your clients.

Equality (Fair treatment to all)

We've now discussed how appearance and communication are key aspects to providing excellent customer service. One last tidbit that I would like to impart is equal treatment to everyone. Your client who spends $100.00 is just as important as your client who spends $10,000.00. They should both be treated as if they are both spending $1,000,000. All clients deserve honesty, integrity, respect, and a quality product or service.

> *"You will do all right, if you obey the most important law in the Scriptures. It is the law that commands us to love others as much as we love ourselves. But if you treat some people better than others, you have done wrong, and the Scriptures teach that you have sinned."*
>
> — *James 2:8-9 CEV*

Appearance. Communication. Equality. The ACE. card is the key to growing a solid foundation for excellent customer service. Keep these tips close to heart. If a client ever feels devalued, not only will they take their business elsewhere, but they'll also tell all of their friends about the horrible experience. In some cases, they'll take to social media and voice their concerns. I'm certain that, if the doll company who inspired this case study knew that this client that only paid $38.79 was also an author, life coach, and small business consultant, I would've received expeditious responses to my inquiries. Imagine if that email that you decided to ignore was a marketing rep from O Magazine. Or if the new client that just ordered the cheapest item in your inventory is actually reviewer for the New York Times. You never know where your "big break" will come from, so for that reason alone, be proactive and not reactive in a business setting.

When you see a potential problem brewing, face it head on and communicate with your customers. They'll appreciate the integrity even if they disagree with your message. You are your brand. Represent it well and never be afraid to ask for assistance. Most importantly, value your customers—you never know which one of them may be inspired to write a book about you!

Khaos Boss

CANDICE COX

Imagine waking up one day and realizing that the life you are living is not the life that you want to live. For me it happened on a Tuesday in January right before my thirtieth birthday. As I looked in the mirror after brushing my teeth, I saw past the image and into my eyes. They were sad, and I didn't know how long they'd been that way. For the first time in a while, I paused and thought about what was happening in my life. I wasn't happy. My husband and I were more like roommates than lovers, I was overweight to the point of looking frumpy, I hated my job, and I longed for my children to have more than what we were providing for them. Something had to give. It was on this day I made the decision to Keep Healing And Overcoming Struggles (KHAOS) vs continuing the Can't Help Acting Out Severely (CHAOS) behavior.

Stating that I wanted to change was a no brainer; doing it was a different story. Day in and day out I found myself going through the motions of life and making little progress toward becoming a new me. Between talking myself out of the changes needed and falling back into old patterns, I constantly landed on different ends of the spectrum.

For a few months, I allowed myself to have conversations in the mirror about my unhappiness but continued to do nothing about it. I call this my "Emotional Hostage" phase. I was fully aware of my barriers but refused to break free from them. Have you ever been in that space? It's a beast to crawl out of it, but it is during this struggle that you find the lessons and guidance needed to push forward.

Standing again in the mirror one day, I decided to stop myself whenever I felt myself complaining about my life. I took a deep breath and stated, "I will no longer be a victim of my own poor choices." Feeling a little motivated, I added, "I will no longer be a victim of my own poor choices. Emotionally, physically, spiritually, and financially, I will be free. I will be me!"

I ran and grabbed a post-it and scribbled down my first affirmation. I quickly placed it on my mirror and repeated the words over and over as I looked into my eyes. The feeling of determination crept over my body. With confidence, I stated my next affirmation: "This will not be my life. Every day I will make one step in the direction of the life I want to live."

I wrote this affirmation on a post-it and placed it on another part of the mirror. Popping the cap back on the pen, I looked at my two new statements. It was in that moment that I realized I could not change my life if I did not change my mindset. To become the person I felt I was born to be, I had to stop being the person that I was. The grieving process for who I was began.

Once I had a full understanding of the mental over-haul needed to live a life of KHAOS, I sat down and got RAW with me. Getting RAW creates a space to: Realize the issues in your life and the root causes. Admit your role in your situation, and Work through each issue individually.

In the realize step, I created a list of people and habits that were assets and liabilities in my life. It took me days to complete my lists. I avoided the truth because I really didn't want to see it on paper, but I had to—soon, I saw that my liabilities outweighed my assets tremendously. I also realized I had checked out in several areas of my life and I was just existing. I admitted I was depressed and had lost sight of the truth within my truth. At times, I bargained with myself over situations and people that I knew needed to leave my life, trying my best to justify my toxic behavior and patterns with stories of what happened over the years. But with every excuse, I told myself, "This will not be my life. Every day I am moving toward who I am meant to be."

Getting RAW opened a lot of old and hidden wounds from my past. I realized a lot of my coping skills and behaviors started from various moments in my life when I'd been hurt, stressed, or not in control. The memories made me angry and ashamed since I was disappointed with how I had allowed myself to be a victim of my own and other peoples' poor choices over the years. This meant I had to work through it. I had to break FREE!

Breaking FREE (Forgive, Release, Embrace, Elevate) is forgiving yourself or the person who you feel has wronged you in your life. At some point, we must stop allowing the decisions and choices of our past, our own or those of others, to hold us emotionally bonded. People are who they are based off the experiences they have encountered in their lives. Release yourself from guilt, shame, and the decisions you did or didn't make. Life happens but that doesn't mean life has to stop. Embrace who you were, are, and will be with love and compassion. Once we make peace with our barriers we can elevate to a higher level of living.

Breaking FREE, especially the forgive part, was hard for me in the beginning because it forced me to see people through their eyes and not my own. In some cases, I wanted people to be all bad with no justification for their actions. This would allow me to just be mad at them for hurting me. But I had to forgive them for being who they were and forgive myself for allowing their actions to bind me emotionally. It's unfair to me to live mentally in a place that is vacant of growth. For this reason, I evicted my failures and bought into my dreams!

Today, I RESET before making decisions in my life: Realize Every Situation Encourages Thought! This skill allows you to take the time to think before you act, react, or assume. It's not fair for you to be a victim of your own poor choices. Bad things do happen to good people and to people who continuously make bad choices. That's called a consequence. RESET taught me how to own my story and to stop blaming others for the pitfalls in my life.

The KHAOS mindset has been a game changer in my life. It is not what I do—it's who I am. Being human, I know there are some situations—bad relationship, not being noticed at your job, more bills than money, etc.—that make you want to live in a state of CHAOS. But you must realize that where you are going is much more reward-ing than where you have been. Admit there are lessons in your struggles and you must make time to pay attention. Work through the things that have you trapped in emo-tional bondage by breaking FREE! Forgive everyone in your life who has taken a part of you and caused damage (that includes yourself). Release patterns and behaviors that are toxic to you and those around you. Embrace your whole self as you are with love and compassion. Tell your-self every day, "Who you were, who you are, and who you will be all represent the magnificent essence of you!" Ele-vate to a higher level of living by spending more time with you, living a life of purpose on purpose, and being patient with yourself!

Being PATIENT allows the opportunity to process through your actions and reactions before responding to a situation. When making a decision, pause and think about what is happening inside and around you. Take notice to when and why you lose your balance in life. Inhale and exhale deeply and slowly to find your balance and to adjust to the situations in your life that cause dis-cord. Think of perspectives beyond your own since your truth is not the only truth at all times. When you are ready to deal with situations that cause discord, tell yourself to now talk, tackle, or tap it out. If you can't talk about it or tackle the tasks needed to handle the situation, tap out to RESET your mind: Remember Every Situation Encourages Thought. There are some situations that you can deal with now, some later, some never. Everything doesn't deserve a response. Remind yourself that it is not okay to hurt yourself on purpose.

I transitioned from a life of CHAOS to KHAOS and have lived amazingly every day since 2012. One of the first steps I took was to change my eating habits. Losing weight wasn't about looking good; it was about truly feeling good. During my weight loss journey, I not only shed physical pounds but also emotional weight. I realized, eating well and exercising started in the mind, not the body, so I had to RESET before I made food and overall life choices.

By taking the time to Remember Every Situation Encourages Thought, I also broke free from the emotional hold my job had on me by truly stepping out on faith. For years, I believed I had to work for someone to fulfill my dreams, now I know that is far from the truth. Quitting wasn't easy as my husband and I separated for a while in April of 2012 and I found myself parenting and living alone for the first time. Scared but ambitious, I started applying to the insurance panels where my clients were members and I began to build my case load as a trauma-informed licensed clinical social worker. After months of constant building, I found myself at a point where my side hustle became my main grind and my job became a side hustle. Once I had three months worth of living expenses saved, I put in my one month notice and transitioned fully into private practice. My motivation was to create an environment where individuals felt safe and unjudged as they learned how to Keep Healing And Overcoming Struggles.

After I found myself in my career, I decided it was time to address my marriage. Almost a year had gone by and the space created a larger gap between my husband and I since we didn't know how to create a new normal with a piece of our hearts missing. We loved each other too much to be friends but were so broken we didn't know how to start over or continue. One cold day in 2013, my husband and I met at the kitchen table in the home I transitioned myself and our children to and broke FREE. By being upfront and honest about everything, we got to a point where we were able to forgive each other for not being what we needed the other to be during our depressed times. We both had turned on autopilot and emotionally checked out on ourselves and each other. That wasn't fair to either of us, not to mentions the silence and emotional distance pushed us further apart.

We released each other from unrealistic expectations and outlined what we wanted and needed from each other going forward. Through processing, tears, and prayer, we found ourselves in a space where we could embrace our lives as they were in the past and present with love and compassion versus anger and resentment. Seeing each other through clear, non-judgmental eyes gave us the ability to reconnect as a team and elevate to a higher level of living, together. It was never easy but, as I prepare to celebrate my eleventh wedding anniversary, it was worth it. There really isn't anything better in a relationship than waking up next to someone you know loves you unselfishly and unconditionally.

Now five years after my breakdown, I realize that my time of uncertainty was a breakthrough. Everything happens as it should. My life had to fall apart to fall together. As I write these words, I smile since I am now what I want to be when I grow up! I have a private practice, A&A Inspirations, where myself and my team of licensed clinicians provide trauma-informed psychotherapy for children, families, and groups. I have my nonprofit, KHAOS, Inc. where my team and I create environments where individuals can become the experts of their own lives as they learn skills to heal and grow. Everyday, I wake up and plant seeds of empowerment, healing, and growth into the lives of others through programs, trainings, retreats, etc. I often feel like I'm living a dream because I get paid to do what I love to do.

I have learned that no matter what happens to you in your life, you cannot give up. What do you have going for you? Waking up with breath in your lungs, movement of your limbs, and the ability to make choices—these small things you may take for granted, if appreciated, can actually change your reality. You cannot change situations that have passed but you can change how you react to them moving forward. If you've lost someone important, take them with you in your heart every day and do not allow their whole lives to live in their final moments. If someone has hurt you, know that hurt people hurt people and choose yourself over their demise. Take the time to see people for who and what they are and make a choice to either deal with them or move on. You cannot change people. People must change themselves. Know your worth and stand on it! There is no room to bargain. Do not discount yourself for anyone, including you!

Life is challenging on its own, but poor choices, environmental barriers, financial struggles, and relationships make things much harder. This is especially the case when you are trying to make sense of all the expectations and responsibilities placed on you. Although things may weigh you down, please know that you can break free of being held emotionally hostage by your situation. Only you can pull yourself out of emotional and mental anguish!

KHAOS Mantra: To live a life of KHAOS, break FREE from your barriers, get RAW with your issues, RESET your mind, and be PATIENT with you.

Each capitalized word is a skill, and each skill is a tool to achieve mental wellness. There is no specific order to learning and living the KHAOS mindset—what's more important is to have the skills in your mental wellness toolkit if and when you need them. You already have everything you need to be who you were designed to be.

Remember, mental wellness is DOPE (Done On Purpose Everyday). Start believing in you and act like the BOSS that you are! You got this! #KHAOSmindset

Below is an activity to help you implement the KHAOS mindset in your own life .

Emotional Hostage: A person who is trapped inside of their head, reliving and relating current situations to past experiences. This causes the individual to repeatedly re-experience uncomfortable emotions and/or reactions of the past.

We are all victims of being held emotionally hostage by the thoughts in our head. There are some thoughts we move past and others that we tuck back in the furthest part of our memory because they bring back feelings of shame, fear, helplessness, grief, abandonment, and other uncomfortable sentiments. You are not alone! We must get RAW with the things that are holding us back from becoming our true selves. Let's work together to get you where you want to be!

Realize: What is holding you emotionally hostage?

Take some time, no less than fifteen minutes, and think about all the people, situations, and experiences that hold you emotionally hostage.

Admit: Why do you allow these things to cloud your mind with toxic thoughts and lead you to unhealthy decisions?

This one may be a little hard. You may have to admit that you hold onto things because the fear of moving past them is scarier than dealing with it as you have been.

Work: Today is a new day!

Even if it has the residue from days past attached to it, today is still a new day! Make the decision to release yourself from barriers that hold you back from living out your purpose. Start with thinking, speaking, and believing this mantra: I will no longer be a prisoner of my own mind. Emotionally, physically, financially, I will be free. I will be ME!

List three emotional hostage-takers and what you will gain from breaking free. Set a date of freedom, and every day, do one positive thing to push yourself toward your goals. When you start to feel held down by your past, close your eyes, take a deep breath, repeat your mantra, and focus. You got this!

Emotional Hostage-Taker:	Gain from Breaking Free:	Done	Due Date
		☐	[Date]
		☐	[Date]
		☐	[Date]

Purposeful Boss

KEYA MCCLAIN

Purpose: The reason for which something is done or created or for which something exists.

My existence, my intentions, my life's happiness is all tied to my purpose. My purpose became more clear, vivid, and undeniable when heartbreak, pain, loss, and disappointment knocked the wind out of me. In this chapter, I will tell you about how my life was when I did not know what my purpose was, when and how I discovered it, and how I've embraced it from thereon. By reading about my experiences, I hope that you are captivated, encouraged, energized, and empowered to seek your purpose and live your dreams.

My very first heartbreak and loss happened when my uncle passed from pancreatic cancer. He was more like my father, and although I lost him over twenty years ago, his presence is still instrumental in my life. In the Veterans Administration Hospital in St. Louis, Missouri, he pulled me in and whispered in my ear "I love you. I want you to be great. You are beautiful and so smart. Finish school, raise Corey, and get married. I want you to be happy, niecey." Every time I wanted to give up I replayed his words in my head.

My next major loss was that of my best friend and brother nearly twenty years later. Very soon after my brother's death, illness plagued me. Shortly after that, my son faced some serious legal issues. Then, my personal life changed even more drastically (second divorce, another death, major surgery). All of this made me want to simply give up. However, with death and challenge comes life and I was soon renewed in my faith.

But first, I had to decide to live my truth and face my obstacles. I could no longer keep layering more hurt and pain over the existing bruises, scars, and bumps. I had to nurse these wounds properly. I had to be accountable for my decisions and actions and start the rehab process. More than anything, I had to accept my past, and then learn, grow, and help others through my stories and transparency. A new me was on the verge of emerging.

I went into a deep and private place with God. I had to remain prayerful, get closer, and meditate. It was through my mediation that I gained more clarity and understanding. As a result, I built a solid foundation within myself. Soon, the siding and roof were formed, and I gained wholeness in who I am. It was a DIY project for my transition. And this transition, in turn, became transformative as I realized the reasons for which I was created and now exist.

For as long as I can remember, I have been inquisitive, always thoroughly breaking down thoughts in my head. As a child, I didn't realize this translated to being analytical. However, those around me noticed how descriptive

I'd get and how I was able to dissect things presented to me. Over the years, people would approach me with information and ask my thoughts and/or ideas. I was often told that I could teach because of how I analyzed and formed opinions or clear summaries; in fact, I tutored my peers in middle school in various subjects.

As a child, I had not understood purpose. I was never taught about purpose or had even heard the word, but I always felt "different." I'd talk to my peers and the things they said weren't similar to my thoughts or desires. My circumstances affected my dreaming, let alone sharing those dreams. My environment, the media, and even the music didn't foster or nurture me enough to understand it all. Although my mom was extremely loving and nurturing, she was not able to identify certain things in me or even know how to empower me to work in those gifts.

For all those parents out there, I encourage you to encourage your children or any child you encounter. Though my mother has learned and now supports everything I do, she didn't know how to do that during my childhood because she herself didn't receive that help from her own mother. However, can you imagine what I would have accomplished earlier in life with that encouragement and support? We can't repeat damaging cycles and make excuses for them, and I truly appreciate my mother for her willingness to understand this. Recognize the light in your children or young people around you and help them explore ways to grow and excel.

Now returning to adulthood, I knew I had to share the pain, loss, and disappointment I felt from all of the deaths and challenges I survived. This was a part of my purpose—to help others, touch others, reach others to the depths of their core. At first, I did not select this path. I did not want to share my personal business or be vulnerable. I did not want to appear too strong, too weak, too much, too bold, too confident, too positive, too empowered, too put together, too perfect, too bad, too unprepared. I tried over and over to run and hide from this gift. In the beginning, I wouldn't even call it a gift. I would down-play it as something I enjoyed as a hobby or a volunteer activity. I would even go down a level to fit in with those who were not in the same space I was in. That was until I embraced all of who I was.

It was over ten years ago when I was told by several people that I was not living my "true purpose." It was difficult for me to see what others saw in me since I had not embraced my gifts and my confidence level was not there. I would be enthralled in supporting others and helping them pursue their purpose, but I was always staying behind the scenes myself. I ran, hid, and ignored for as long as I could (or I thought I was). Well, you can delay, but you can't deny. My purpose chased me down, stayed on my heels until I embraced it.

I grew and learned over time. I am expected to reach many lives and be the reason others don't quit, and I feel I've been given another chance to embrace my gifts and take a ton of risks. I believe in my purpose and dreams despite the naysayers or nonbelievers. I encourage myself even if I'm the only one in the bleachers and on the field. I don't deny my truth. If you sit still, listen, believe, pray, and meditate to hear from Your Source, you will move forward. Live out your purpose and fulfill those dreams. Quiet yourself, listen, and be obedient to that feeling. Your purpose is just on the other side! And remember: do not to give the naysayers and Negative Nelly's a first row seat. It is time to eliminate dream killers, vision vampires, and goal grinches. This is probably one of the most valuable pieces of advice I can give you. Why? Because if you listen long enough to the bad talk, you will believe it and it will be on repeat in your mind, creating self-doubt, negative self-talk, and unnecessary comparisons of yourself to others. If you cannot eliminate those people form your vicinity, at least decrease contact with them.

"Carefully watch your thoughts, for they become your words. Manage and watch your words, for they will become your actions. Consider and judge your actions, for they have become your habits. Acknowledge and watch your habits, for they shall become your values. Understand and embrace your values, for they become your destiny."
—Mahatma Gandhi

As a pre-teen/teen, we all start considering our futures and what we want to do. I had a dream of singing like Whitney

Houston. I entered a talent show at school and the result was not what I wanted or even anticipated. I practiced with my friends and classmates for weeks, but I didn't win. But losing the talent show was not what crushed my confidence level—it was what others said about me and what I believed. They were mean and teased me for weeks, so I stopped singing after that. As the years went by, very few people knew I loved to sing or could even sing. I had been extremely passionate about this dream, but I had a hard time pursuing it after that incident. Soon, singing dissipated completely and new dreams were envisioned.

The next dream that came into play was created from a positive image displayed on television. I admired Claire Huxtable on The Cosby Show and aspired to become an attorney like her. My last year in high school, I made a decision to go out of state for college and law school. However, fear crept back in as those same voices of doubt returned and decided against college out of state. Eventually, I became pregnant with my one and only son at eighteen, and again, gave up on dreaming. I got a job, enrolled in the local community college, and got an apartment. The dreams of being a lawyer changed to "I'll be a paralegal because I'm a new mom and law school would be too difficult" (there's that self-doubt again).

Ultimately, I obtained my associates and paralegal certificate and later went on to obtain a bachelor of arts in legal studies and master of arts in legal analysis from Webster University in St. Louis, Missouri. After calculating my student loan debt and time vested, I realized that law school had been definitely possible, if only I had tried. It was a crushing blow—I had cheated myself again, or so I thought. But soon, I realized that the path I followed was completely necessary for a number of reasons.

Sometimes, certain experiences are necessary to get you to your intended destination. I started adding all my experiences up: attending school, working a full-time job, being a wife and then ex-wife, a young mother, student, mentor, mentee, and professional. The experience of serving others on boards at schools and with various organizations had catapulted me into leadership positions. These all added up to lengthy and valuable experience that would all serve me and those I am called to serve. I ultimately took those experiences and the knowledge acquired to work in my purpose. Although it wasn't apparent during those seasons of doubt, my purpose became clear after the smoke cleared. If you are questioning your current position, you too, may simply be getting positioned to use those experiences to empower someone else.

But let's go back to when I hadn't realized all this yet. Through the years, I have worked at some of the largest and most reputable law firms, the United States District Court, and Fortune 500 companies. None of these accomplishments gave me the happiness I sought and felt I deserved. It wasn't until I began volunteering at my church, speaking to young people, motivating others, taking a phone call from a friend or family member who needed inspiration, and seeing transformations take place that I realized what living one's dreams actually feels like.

I realized that I was happy to serve others, instruct, inspire, and motivate others. It was through this awareness that I really understood and completely embraced my gifts . I now make this my work. I was met with negativity, judgment, and lack of understanding by some, but I also had a great deal of people who supported and believed in the pursuit of my purpose. Be sure to keep positive, successful, empowered, and supportive people around you. If you allow negativity into your space, it will eat away at you. Do not focus on those who don't support you. This really was one of the hardest things for me, but ultimately, those people didn't really relate to my purpose. As a mother protects her children, you must protect the energy you allow in your space. Your dreams do not extend to others and it is not their responsibility to cultivate you. Instead, find a personal team who shares and supports your vision.

While I excavated my purpose, my creativity became my refuge. I found solitude in writing and recognized the same in my son. He was not much of a verbally expressive kid but he was a vibrant writer and thinker. The summer before my son entered high school, I enrolled him in a Corner Pocket Writing Workshop at the Missouri History Museum, not realizing that it would be life-changing for us both. I was in awe of his transformation and his blooming confidence. He soon began to trust his gift.

Watching my teenage son, I was inspired. A series of events led me to write more and share what I had written over the years. Years earlier, I started writing a book and never completed it. It was more of an autobiography, but doubt, fear, and distrust of my gifts led me to tuck away yet another dream. However, I started attending an open mic night through my son's writing workshop. The first night I was there, I knew I had to share my writing. I quickly began reciting poetry I previously wrote and then wrote new poems and stories. I did this for about five years consistently and published my first book of poetic healing, *My Words Healed My Soul*, in April 2016. I quickly began working on my second book of poetry and a book on leadership. The poetry book, *The Depths of My Soul Healed Through Love and Empowerment*, was published just a year later in April 2017, and the leadership book was realized in fall 2017. I am also a coauthor in an upcoming poetry collection. Once I saw that my powerful, honest, and transparent messages were able to engage various audiences, I was pushed further along in my journey to purposefulness.

More and more, I gained confidence in my skills and gifts, and even more so in my dreams. I mentioned earlier in the chapter that I felt like I had wasted time going to college and never getting to law school. I also mentioned how I tutored others when I was younger and was told that I should teach. When I attended a vision board conference, my desires manifested. I realized that I wanted to teach professionally in the legal field and specifically to those who have little to no experience working in professional environments. An opportunity presented itself to teach paralegal courses, and again, this would become a part of my purposeful journey.

At around the same time, I began being called on by many to speak about how I was making my shift from being a legal assistant to teaching legal work. So a few years ago, I formed my nonprofit organization, Empower2Be, a women's empowerment organization whose vision is to maximize positive experiences among women while encouraging this generation to pour that same seed into the next generation. The motivation to start the nonprofit came from my own negative thoughts and experiences about women relationships in the past. I always had more male friends in the past, but when I lost my best male friend, so many women came together to love and support me. Additionally, I met a friend who introduced me to her circle of friends. I was embraced and held by sisters.

In the past, my experience with women were not so open and receptive so I was shocked, yet happy to be a part of this sisterhood. I realized that all my experiences had not been bad, but instead, I had been putting out a defensive and stand-off energy that was attracting the same. I learned through positive, empowering, and loving friendships that women need each other and we can do amazing things together.

What started as a Facebook group of women to share motivational and inspiring quotes became an organization full of women who are loving, kind, supporting, and empowered. We have bonded, networked, and established friendship through the conferences and workshops I've hosted. Through this work, I recognized yet another gift: coaching. Women seek deep guidance and assistance when achieving their goals and recognizing their gifts. Many of them came to me for this guidance and I realized I was resonating and connecting with many. My experiences, education, and knowledge now translate to my life-coaching services, which focus primarily on women. However, I serve anyone who reaches out to me—I work with all who are ready to get into action and live out their purpose by providing strategies that will create long-term success.

The decision to quit my job as a legal assistant was fearful, yet empowering. I was excited and nervous at the same time. But you know you are working in your purpose when things begin to align themselves perfectly. You meet and connect with the right people who will help you elevate to the next level. I have met people from all over who would then connect with me months later, because I resonated with them and they remembered the connection we made, partnerships we formed, ideas we shared, and opportunities we presented.

I am so glad that I chose to pursue my passion and purpose, and persevere through to the next level. But always remember: when you are working in your purpose, there is never an end date or a success big enough to make you stop or get comfortable. My biggest lesson was not allowing negative chatter, lack of support from friends and family, and limiting beliefs to prevent me from living out my purpose. I changed my thoughts about myself from negative to positive and learned not to take everything personally or to place limitations on what I can achieve.

Through hearing my story, obstacles, and breakthroughs, I hope that you've taken away a few lessons. However, the most important lesson is that you were born with purpose. If you are now exploring or taking steps toward fulfilling your purpose I encourage you to first take time to reflect quietly. Secondly, use your pain and obstacles as lessons. Thirdly, trust your gifts. Lastly, connect with like-minded individuals; get a mentor and hire a coach.

From one purposeful boss to many others, you have the power! Be focused, driven, consistent, and diligent in pursuing your purpose.

Purpose-Driven Boss

Tonita Smith

Giving Birth to Purpose

Do you know what it's like to live most of your adult life doing the same mundane routine? Working hard at your job day-to-day just to pay bills, but not being happy? It's kind of like having a plastic bag over your head and feeling your breath and life being drained from your body. You have the power to remove the bag at any time but, for some reason, you can't find the strength to lift your hands. Your mind and body are in a state of paralysis. How does one get to this point? More importantly, how does one get out of that space?

I grew up in the era where you were taught to go to school, get good grades, graduate, get a good job, work hard, get married, raise your family, retire one day, if you're lucky—and then what? Nobody ever told me what was supposed to come after that. There absolutely had to be more to life then this old-school way of thinking. Working hard and living paycheck to paycheck is not living life. I wanted to experience what everybody on television or outside of my circle talked about, living life to the fullest. The Good Life!

I was thirty-five-years old, had failed at two marriages, and found myself raising three sons alone. What was I supposed to do now? I was in the Army, which was very stressful and demanding. I was barely staying above water. I didn't feel like there was another way out, and getting out of the military after serving over six years was not an option—we needed the benefits and the security that the government offered. I had so many hopes and dreams for myself, but with everything going on, those dreams felt so farfetched.

Day in and day out, I worked long hours, maintained a household, and raised growing boys—this was not my idea of living. To top it off, we were living in a state where there was no family around to offer support. I did what I had to do as a mother and sat on my gifts, never to unwrap them because I didn't think it was possible to add yet another thing to my cup that was already running over.

As my sons got older and became more independent, I began to see myself doing more of what I loved. I was still fearful to take a giant leap, so I played it safe with simple entrepreneurial ventures like experimenting with a MLM company and selling knock-off handbags. The money from the side hustle was nice, plus I had the opportunity to meet lots of new women.

At this point, I had served sixteen years in the military on active duty with little or no control over my life. Don't get me wrong, the government has been good to me. I earned my bachelor's of science degree as a registered nurse and a master's degree in nursing as a nurse educator. There have been more accomplishments in between the schooling than I can even count. I'm grateful and not complaining; however, beyond the titles and degrees, "now what" and "so what" remained. For me, these questions came out of nowhere, perhaps after my sons went out on their own. I truly thought I would be happy and content at this point.

But one day, the light bulb went off: I realized that I was over the green suit, I was no longer happy or content with my current profession, and I wanted to do so much more than a side hustle. I wasn't just ready to climb outside the box, I was ready to jump out of it. What had been holding me back for so long? Was it being a mom? Fear? Doubt? Procrastination? After all, I was so passionate and very good at being more than just a mom, wife, soldier, and army nurse.

Some may say, "Those are great accomplishments! What's the problem?" I would answer by saying honestly that, while I served my country proudly and honorably, I was over it. There was much more to me than the uniform and titles I wore. Despite being a nurse, I didn't feel like I was helping many people or making a real difference. This was no longer comfortable for me.

My Light Bulb Moment

I was afforded the opportunity to return to school full-time while remaining on active duty. I thought that maybe going back to get another degree would be enough to fulfill my entrepreneurial void. Boy, was I wrong. Then, came along my third and final husband who just happened to be a full-time entrepreneur. God knew exactly who and what I needed at that time. I always say that God has a great sense of humor. My husband is one of my greatest gifts and He showed me that he is connected to my destiny.

I've always had a love for fashion and accessories. I would often joke and say that I wear a uniform by day but have a whole other life by night. The military is not about fashion and it believes in "dress right dress," meaning everyone must look the same. You don't get to be creative or different since we all wear the exact same uniform. The military says that you were not meant to stand out but I always thought: Why fit in when you were meant to stand out?

One day, God gave me the vision to start my own online accessory boutique. I think the idea started when I began posting pictures online of myself in different outfits and receiving an overwhelming number of comments, likes, and messages asking, "Girl, where did you get that dress from? That necklace? That scarf?" I'd tell them where I purchased my ensemble, down to the price I paid. That was when God gave me a vision: why not sell the things you like to wear, continue wearing them, post pictures, and share the fashion? I could easily link the pieces in my outfit to my own website and help other women look and feel great! That's exactly what I did.

I prayed and asked God who I should collaborate with because, as you know, the efforts of two are far better than the efforts of one any day. God spoke to me clear as day and said, "Your cousin, LaSonya." My cousin and I grew up in the same household like sisters, both of us admiring each other's different but unique style. In fact, she went to college for fashion design, so the partnership was perfect. God is Good, right? Yes, He is! This was the birth of our online boutique, Fashion Remix Boutique: "When All Else Fails, Accessorize."

I love being an entrepreneur and sharing my gifts so freely with others. The more I attend networking events or participate in vendor events, what I do feels less like work. But as much as I love it, I realized that having a boutique wasn't the final niche for me. In fact, it was just the itch I needed to scratch to open so many other doors that were waiting to be sprung open all along. The more I met other entrepreneurs and like-minded dope women, the more I saw myself doing more and sharing more. I was pregnant with my real passion and I needed to give birth by serving others through inspiration, motivation, and empowerment.

It all starts with identifying your true passion and keeping God in the center; in His timing, He will show you ways to monetize your passion so it never feels like work. This is my best season yet and I know that the best is yet to come. I never had to wait until my sons were adults to do this! Boy, did I feel like I wasted a lot of time, but the truth is, there is not such thing as time wasted. It is always about God's perfect timing, my preparation for my future.

And Then This

God has allowed me to unwrap and accept so many of my gifts. In fact, I'm amazed to be positioned with several visions and thankful to be able to put them all to work: "Faith without works is dead" (James 2:14). God can give the vision but vision without movement is just a dream. Visions with hard work can equal multiple streams of income—this is how the rich get rich and stay rich. That's why I don't forgo my initial vision to enter the military: I will continue to serve until I qualify for retirement and work hard in preparation for that day. When I reach twenty years, I will transition into my passion and everything that my husband and I are building now; the only difference is, my new work will be on a full-time basis and I will have the freedom that I have longed for.

You may be asking yourself, "So, did she just wake up one day and the light bulb was on? Or did she just decide that 'today was going to be the day that she would become her own boss?" No, not exactly. But once I realized my purpose, not only was the light bulb on, but flashing lights and sirens followed. For too long they were screaming, "What have you been waiting on?" For too long I was like so many others, afraid to move because of fear of failure. But I have never heard of any great person who became great while sitting in their comfort zone.

I told my husband for five years that, one day, I would write a book. I said I would write a children's books, but God had other plans for me. My first book, *The Power of*

Shut-up Grace was birthed from my test to my testimony, and it's a book for people of all ages to learn from my struggle. I put my power into words. The Bible says, "Life and death are in the power of the tongue and they that that love it shall eat the fruit thereof" (Proverbs 18:21). Your own words can breed positive or negative outcomes over your life. That's deep.

Well, after the birth of the book, something magical happened. Magic called "Opportunities." I wasn't really putting myself out there to get noticed, just your regular social media stuff because I still had to adhere to military regulations twenty-four hours a day. But I soon began receiving emails and texts asking me to speak at events. I never saw myself as a motivational speaker. I had always been someone my family or friends called for advice or to vent to because they trusted that I would give them the raw truth through God's love—I quickly realized that, through those moments, God was preparing me for the future.

Now, I want to be ready to receive anything that God has for me. I buried fear, doubt, and procrastination some time ago; instead, I pray for guidance, then accept opportunities as they come along. With every opportunity, God elevates me a little bit higher in my craft and in Him. There are times that I find myself crying out to the Lord because I'm in awe of His goodness and favor. All I can say is that there are benefits in staying in God's will. I trust Him with everything.

I've been fortunate to meet, network, and collaborate with some trailblazing women. I soon found myself in the position of being consulted on many topics such as how to start a boutique, how to write a book, and how to maintain a healthy relationship when your tongue is sharp as a sword. I eventually became a bit overwhelmed because, remember, I was still serving full-time on active duty and pursuing these other passions on the side.

Okay, I was now walking in my purpose, but now I needed to find my balance. I decided to hire a business coach to help me weave my great passions together to produce results that would help me while serving others. This was one of the best decisions that I've made in business. You must recognize when you need help and be willing to seek out that help from the right person or people. This can be tricky, so do your research! YouTube is okay for some things, but not everything is not a DIY project, especially when it comes to your business. You are your brand and how others see your brand says a lot about you and your credibility. You can get far with the right people, so always pray for divine connections.

Did you think I was done telling you about my passions? After I achieved balance, I wrote my second book, *The Power of a Purpose-Driven Woman*. This project was heartfelt, because up until recent, I had been a woman with great ideas that never came to fruition because I was too afraid to fail. I played it safe as a nine-to-five girl, trading dollars for time. Now, I have the pleasure of helping other women identify their own purpose and bury fear, doubt, and procrastination so they can walk in their greatness. To do this, there are layers that we must peel back before we can get to the core. Each client takes a confidence self-assessment which is offered free on my website. Next, they schedule an one-on-one mentoring session with me or they purchase other products and services that I offer because they still may be on the ledge but not ready to totally jump—this is okay too!

I also mentor youth through a violence prevention project that focuses on helping children who have been exposed to violence, indirectly and directly. This project is near and dear to my heart because young people are our future leaders, doctors, lawyers, caregivers, and more. The youth in this program are taught anger management skills, coping skills, the importance of education, and conflict resolution. We must be examples of the change we desire to see.

Did I mention that I didn't remove any of my former hats when I became an entrepreneur? I am still a wife, mother of three adult sons, and a grandmother of four grandchildren. My husband and I also buy, sell, renovate, and rent investment property via Smith's Homes LLC. Yes, add landlord to my resume, too! I am all about multiple sources of income and you should be too. If there is a will, God will make a way. Do you have the heart to serve others? If you have the faith to believe it, be willing to do the work to achieve it. Remember, everything is about your mindset: if you think you can't, you can't and you won't. If you say it's too hard, it'll be even harder. But if you can think and believe it, you can achieve it.

Lastly, my friends, I would love to stay connected with you—I encourage you to live life to the fullest by identifying your purpose so that you can walk in your greatness. God bless you, and thank you for allowing me to share my journey to purpose.

As a mentor, here are some declarations I share with my mentees:

> Everyone is good at something. Identify what you love and what you're good at and find a way to create a business around it.

> You can accomplish anything if you are willing to put your heart and soul into doing.

> Fear, doubt, and procrastination do not travel on the road to success. Remember, God allows U-turns, so don't be afraid or ashamed to turn around and run in the right direction.

> Speak life and blessings over your business, your plans, and your dreams. Next, roll up your sleeves and do the work.

> Stay away from toxic people. Surround yourself with three winners and eventually you will become the fourth winner.

Never stop reading and learning new things. Reset your mind for renewal—it may take a different strategy to get where you want to go.

Don't be afraid to try. You will never know how great you can be if you never take that very first step.

God gives us the spirit of faith, not fear.

Move intentionally and purposefully in everything you do.

Create a life that you don't need a vacation from.

Mindset Boss

LUBERTA LYTLE

Life will throw all kinds of obstacles your way, but you must keep your eyes on the prize. My life journey has had its fair share of ups and downs, but each setback has made me more determined to keep pushing. Today, I work with women who are stuck and comfortable, but have a desire to move and get comfortable with being uncomfortable, so they may start building a legacy for themselves and their family.

The change starts with your mindset about what you really desire for your life. Mindset is defined in the dictionary as, "an attitude, disposition, or need and/or an intention or inclination." I generally express to clients, friends, and family that, if you want to make a change in your current situation, you must first start by changing your mindset. If you are looking for a different response or answer, then you must look deep into yourself. If the situation remains the same, then your mindset has not changed. Humans are in control of how their lives turn out. If you are one of those people who speaks negatively about everything in your life, then your life will be nothing but misery, despair, heartache, and unhappiness. We get out what we put in.

So if you truly desire to change your life, then start with how you speak over every aspect of it. Negative words and actions will result in a negative life. Positive words and action will cause a shift of positivity. Remember, we are truly in control of the outcome of our lives, so to make those necessary changes, start with how you speak about yourself and your circumstances. If you don't make it difficult for yourself, changing your mindset can be a pretty simple process.

Changing the mindset seems more challenging for women, due to the simple fact that we have become accustomed to just "going with the flow" of daily life. A male-dominated society has told women to stay in the household as a housewife instead of getting a "real" job, whether it's a nine-to-five or a side business. We've been told that our thoughts and opinions are not valued, and we must not desire or hope for better lives. We've been told that anything we receive within our household, we should thank our significant other for. We've been told to believe that we should not walk in our divine purpose or live out our dreams. Generally speaking, women have been told that they should be seen and not heard. So, as per what they're told, women often make the packaging look pretty and put together on the outside, and live in hell on the inside.

Women have accepted this type of treatment—until now. If you look at the world now, gender roles and responsibilities are changing because, over the last few years, women have become more vocal in the entrepreneurial world and within their households. Women are creatures that can birth babies, run households, and companies, plus anything else thrown her way. But women, even with all of the skills and creativity, at times will diminish their light so others' lights will shine, and sit out of the game on the sidelines. We remain strong, independent human beings, even when we just want someone to help solve and/or make our problems better. People forget sometimes that even the strongest person can suffer too!

To help them assert their rights as women further, I tell my clients these five tenets during their first coaching session:

1. Change your mindset in order to change your life.

2. Believe in yourself. If you do not believe in you, why should anyone else believe in you?

3. Activate your faith.

4. Pray Until Something Happens (PUSH).

5. Trust the process.

Women wear many hats and titles, but we must remember that we too have a divine calling and purpose for our lives: mother, wife, sister, daughter, chauffer, or any other title they want to attach to our names are just that—titles. They do not define who we truly are and what we are called to do. Women have been misled to believe that they cannot have it all and be successful. Guess what? You can have it all, plus be more than you ever dreamed you could be.

My true ah-ah moment came at the age of fifty. I was told by my co-workers, ex-husband, current husband, friends, and family that I should be content with working for the State of Illinois. Has this job taken care of my family? Yes, it has. Has this job given me opportunities to advance? Yes, it has. Has this job given me security? Yes, it has. And that's why I've remained employed with this organization for thirty years. I've been promoted and even returned to school to further my education. But something had been missing for the last ten years. What was missing was my divine purpose. My job just wasn't it! It was just something that gave me security to become comfortable and complacent instead of growing. I listened and accepted what others said about me working for this organization, hoping that the void inside me would just go away. Well, I'm here to tell you that it never happened. I've known for about ten years that I should be working with women to empower, motivate, and inspire. But, instead of going in this direction, I decided to just ignore it and go in the opposite direction.

My story truly resembles the Bible story of Jonah. Jonah, chapters 1-4 give the following description of how Jonah ignored what God called him to do and the price he paid for being disobedient: Jonah knew that God had given him specific instructions for his assignment, but he decided to reroute and change the plans. Still, in the end,

God still received the glory despite Jonah's disobedience. The amazing thing about God is that He will allow you to run in the opposite direction, make mistakes, and still wait on you to realize that you need His help to complete the task. So, most of the time when you are going through a trial or test, God is actually preparing you for your testimony. He hopes that you will pass this situation, and if not, He will continue presenting the same test.

I compare this with taking my state licensing exam. I started taking the exam and noticed that the same type of questions kept popping up on the computer screen. The exam is set up in a way that, if you are within a certain margin of failing, then the question will continue in that particular area until you reach the true pass of failing and/or you start answering the question correctly. Only then does the exam move onto another area.

God loves us so much that he will continue to give us the same test until we reach the passing mark, so that we can move onto the next phase of our life. We must realize that when we want or desire something new, we must be made new. Even if the choices you make and the turns you take are wrong, God will allow it, because He already knows that you will eventually get back on the right path. In fact, you must get back on the right path.

It does not matter how much education you obtain and/or how many promotions you receive. If you are called to fulfill a specific duty, it will keep a void in your life until you fill that duty. You can run, but you cannot hide. I was in denial and ignored my divine calling, but I finally surrendered last year. My divine calling is not working for the State of Illinois, obtaining my bachelor of science in organizational leadership, nor receiving my master of business in administration. Those accolades are fine and good, but the void in my life still remained. My divine calling is working with women who desire more out of their lives. I receive great joy helping, supporting, and encouraging women to move out of their comfort zone. But in order for me to do that, I too had to step out of my comfort zone and turn my dream into a reality.

Women are one of the most flexible creatures that God has placed on this earth. We spend so much time ensuring that everyone else lives and fulfills their dreams, but are quick to make excuses regarding our own dreams. Here are some of the excuses we use as to why we cannot or should not start walking in our purpose:

I am too busy.

My family needs me.

The time is not right.

I will wait until the kids grow up.

I will wait until my significant other finishes reaching their goal.

We could use the money for something else.

No one wants to hear what I have to say.

I am not smart enough to start my own business.

That type of business has already been established.

I will not be successful.

When we come up with these excuses (which is what they really are), we sell ourselves short and deprive ourselves of living a more fulfilling life. Each and every day, women make the impossible possible in their households. And yet, we allow time to slip away from us by not taking the steps needed to start walking in our divine purpose. We fail to realize that, when we release and activate our divine purpose, we actually come in alignment with our calling.

We are called to serve people obediently, which gives God the glory. When we share our stories, testimonies, tragedies, and triumphs, we leave legacies to our families, encouraging others to step out of their comfort zone and grow instead of remaining complacent. Our good and bad situations must be shared with others to help them realize that they too can overcome those particular obstacles in their lives. Still, what do most of us tend to do? We keep those things inside and pray that no one finds out about our situation. The reality is that we've all been through something in our lives. If you can help ease someone's pain and misery by sharing your story, it could heal them and you too.

The things that I have shared in this chapter are things I've experienced for myself. I have had to deal with low self-esteem, depression, being told that my thoughts and opinions do not matter, verbal and physical abuse, and low self-confidence. In order for me to start walking in my divine purpose, I had to do two things. First, I had to change my mindset, and second, I had to start believing in myself. If you do not believe, why would anybody else believe in you?

I can and will share my experiences of becoming a teenage mother at the age of fourteen and sixteen. Of losing my mother from breast cancer at the age of twenty-one. Of being a victim of mental and physical abuse. Of divorcing and losing parental custody of my children. Of listening to bad advice from friends and loved ones, who were actually undercover haters trying to stop me from living out your dreams.

I share these stories to show women that they too can overcome their situations. I understand that, when you are depressed, you would prefer to stay in the bed and allow life to pass you by. Still, you must get up and push through it. I understand what it feels like to be told that you are not worthy enough to be loved; instead, you must say, "I know my worth and I love me." I understand that consuming alcohol feels like it will take all of your pain away; however, you must deal with the issues instead of trying to drink them away. I understand why you volunteer for any and everything presented to you, in order to appear very busy, but deep down, you really just want to die. I get it, but sometimes, you just have to dig deep within yourself and decide that you are no longer going to live in fear, but instead live by faith.

In order to live a different life, you must do something different. But the questions are: are you willing to make the necessary sacrifices to achieve this new life or will you continue allowing yourself to live by others rules? You can be or do anything that you set your mind on, but you must be willing to allow your light to shine! I understand that your friends and family may tell you that you are crazy for wanting to step outside of the box in order to live the life that you desire; but it is okay do you, boo!

What does not kill you will make you strong. We are the captains of our lives, so start taking control instead of allowing others to control our life. My life experiences of being a teenage mother, motherless child, victim of domestic violence, divorcee, and victim of low self-confidence are all part of my story, but the story has not ended. I had to experience and overcome all of those tragedies, through hard work and self-recognition. I graduated from high school despite being a teenage mother of two, grieved the loss of my mother, found my inner strength and left an abusive relationship, made peace with my two children who suffered during the divorce, truly discovered myself instead of allowing others' opinions to dictate my thought process, and learned to disregard the opinions of others that are only meant to hurt me. This is how I became the woman I am today.

And even after fifty-two years of living, I am truly pre-paring for the next chapter in my life. We all enjoy living and playing our lives in the safe, comfortable zone. But in the end, are we really living life? It is time for all of us to actual live life instead of allowing life to live us. So, instead of making excuses on why you should not start walking and living in your divine purpose, ask yourself the questions below.

Remember: your faith to succeed in life must be greater than your fear of failing!

What is your "Why?" _____

_____

What gets you excited? _____

_____

What would success feel like? _____

_____

What type of freedom would you achieve? _____

_____

How will you feel when you start walking in your purpose?

_____

_____

Self-Love Boss

NICOLE HARRELL-KELLY

"No weapon formed against me shall prosper, I am more than a conqueror"

—Isaiah 54:17

Being a mom is no easy task, but being a single working mother is a downright challenge. However, it is one of the most rewarding jobs I have ever had the pleasure to hold. I am a divorced, single mother of three. For years, I worked unhappily in the legal field to make ends meet, stayed in relationships well past their expiration dates, and I did it all, I claimed, in the name of love—love for my children, that is. The thing about that is that, even though I saw my children every day, I really didn't know them. How could I when I hadn't taken the time to even know myself at this point in my life?

My children could sense and feel all the tension and unhappiness in my life long before I would acknowledge it to myself. I thought that, because I worked hard and long hours to provide "things" for my kids, they were fine. I believed that, if I stayed with their dad even though I was unhappy, it would give them a sense of security and stability. I was wrong about both those things. I began to see my children acting out to gain my attention. I also began to see and feel the stressful effects of staying in a relationship and a job where I was miserable.

There was a point in my life where I fell in deep despair, thinking that the only reason my relationship wasn't working was because my career was ruining it. My mind was so frazzled that I couldn't see the real reason my life was in shambles. I sat down and took inventory of our relationship and began to acknowledge that I had been unhappy with that man many years before that job ever came in the picture.

Still, I stayed because I had allowed fear to take over. The fear of being alone with three kids and wondering what man would be willing to accept that package deal terrified me. This fear was rooted in the questions my ex would repeatedly ask me: "With three kids, who else do you think will want you?" "You think you can do better than me?" "Who do you think you are, The Queen of England?"

I didn't realize that these questions were just examples of his insecurities anytime he knew he was doing something wrong. At the time, it never occurred to me that I did not have to always defend myself, that I could just leave the relationship if I was going to constantly be under verbal attack. Instead, I let the questions and comments run on a loop through my mind. After hearing these negative statements and so many others like them for the bulk of our fifteen years together, my self-esteem was bruised and damaged. I was so self-conscious I was afraid to make a change in any area of my life. I had allowed him to project his mediocre mentality and perception of himself, as well as his lack of motivation and drive, onto me, and they spilled over into other areas of my life. I was paralyzed from making the changes I needed to achieve success by my standards.

I also remember specifically feeling extremely unhappy in my job, and again, I was too afraid to try something different. Years ago, when I had taken the job, I loved it. However, through the years, that changed. I endured racism and discrimination, and still, I stayed with that firm for more than ten years. I had taken on a mentality that I was lucky to have a job and be able to take care of my children. Since my self-esteem was so low, I was too afraid to even believe in anything better. I convinced myself that, because I went to school for legal studies, surely legal work was how I "should" be helping others. I never took into consideration the toll that job had on my body. I was beginning to have neck and back spasms due to stress and my stomach would feel as though it was being tied in knots whenever I pulled into our office garage. My stress levels were sky high and I couldn't get along with anyone around me. I did not like the person I had become. Fear had taken the place that my purpose was supposed to hold.

I finally went to my physician. He told me honestly, "Nicole, I have been seeing you since you were eighteen and I have never seen you this upset." He suggested that I leave my job, to which I responded, "I can't do that. I have kids to take care of."

But one day, I woke up and admitted to myself just how unhappy I was. Just by admitting that, there was a huge shift in my thinking. I began to remember who I really was and what I wanted. While I admit having a job can be a blessing, once that job puts your health at risk, it is no longer a blessing—rather it is a liability. Nothing that causes you stress and pain consistently is of God, nor should it be considered a blessing.

I also came to see that I had been taught better than to accept poor treatment from anyone, no less a man who was supposed to love and cherish me. My parents didn't break their backs to send me to private school for all those years only for me to squander away every opportunity I had at success, especially for someone who didn't even think that I nor our children deserved better lives. I had lowered my standards to make something work with someone who would never see eye to eye with me. I never intended to stop short and build someone else's dreams and put all my finances at their disposal. I had become subpar and that was unacceptable. That had to end.

I am no longer at that firm and I dropped my toxic relationship. Since leaving, my stress levels are under control, and I am happier and more easy-going than I have been in a long time. My two adult sons love and respect me because they know what I endured to give them a better life. My ten-year-old daughter gets to see a mother who is a confident role model for her and challenges her to be her best. I feel as though all the pressure that I was under were only God's test to prepare me for the great purpose that He has in store. I now realize that I was unhappy before because I had pushed my dreams aside and lost sight of the fact that I am here to live life, not merely exist. Somehow on my way to adulthood and through motherhood and failed relationships, I had lost who I was at the core.

So how did these positive changes and realizations all come about? These positive changes took place after my mother passed away in 2012. I remember standing over her casket with tears running down my face and promising her and myself that I would no longer allow myself to be dragged down, degraded, or disrespected by anyone again. I vowed to build true bonds with my children and to be there more for them, even if it meant that I could no longer get as many material things for them as I had when I worked those crazy hours. I was and am still determined to go after what truly fulfills me and creates happiness in my life and the lives of my children. If the desirable circumstances don't exist, it is in my power to create them.

In order to make positive and conscious changes, I began to sit still and meditate and pray, really listening to my inner voice. As a result, not only did I begin to remember and accept the things that I really want in a man and a career, I began to remember all the dreams and goals that I had for my life. I was now experiencing peace and was able to relax more around friends and family. It no longer felt as though the weight of the world was upon me.

After leaving my job, I wasn't making as much money as I had been in Corporate America, but I had peace of mind and time to focus on the people and things that really mattered to me. Interestingly, even though the paychecks weren't equal to those I received while working, the money that came in was never short when bills were due. God sent me the right blessing on time, every time—it just took me stepping out on faith. I have been able to get my financial situation in order and build my credit scores back up. I have had and continue to have so many divine connections. God just keeps placing me in the right places with the right people seemingly falling onto my path.

In 2016, I published my first book, *Men Don't Always Lie, Sometimes Women Don't Listen*. The book teaches the reader about holding oneself accountable to open doors of self-acceptance and greater possibilities of building the type of relationship(s) they want. This book is in memory of my mother, who always taught my siblings and me that we could do anything we put our minds to. She would point to her head and say, "Once you get it up here, they can never take it away." It took me many years to truly begin to understand what she meant. Now, I see that our thoughts are instrumental in how we see ourselves and how we live out our lives.

Speaking of choosing how we live our lives, this 2016 book discusses my relationship truths and how I learned to love myself and break free from toxic relationships. I share examples of my past relationships as well as a question-answer section provided by men to illustrate how women can better interact with men and build strong and lasting connections. At the time, I was over forty, divorced, and a single mother of three, I felt like I had been through hell and back. I was ready to be the best mother to my children I could possibly be. I was ready for a serious relationship and needed to know the real reason I had not been in one in years. I did some soul searching and journaling and that's when I hit the jackpot. I found and accepted the true meaning behind my heartbreak: I hadn't loved myself enough to follow my own intuition and leave situations where I did not feel that I received the love I deserved. I made the choice to settle for less. I now realize that no one is responsible for my happiness other than me and that I must create the change I want in my life by making more self-loving choices. I come first.

I initially began writing my book as a journal to heal myself from my relationship. God gave me the title of my book once I realized that no matter how those past relationships ended, the men involved were not totally to blame. I had to accept responsibility and be accountable for my choices and actions. Once it was completed, I knew that I had to share my stories because there are so many women in the world who are currently in or have been in situations like mine. These women may believe they are alone; they may feel lost, scared or just plain hurt. I needed them to know that they are not alone.

It was then that I grasped my real passion: to help as many women as I can to know and understand that they are worthy of love and that the first people they deserve to receive it from is themselves. I feel that one of my greatest desires is to help encourage women to truly self-love and be their very best possible self. I want to inspire women to look within to uplift and take charge of their own lives, to be their own cheerleaders first. My writing is meant to empower women to make better choices and to learn and grow from their previous experiences rather than holding on to anger, hurt, and resentment.

While it may seem like I am all over the place from parenthood to intimate relationships, career to health, I want you to understand that all of these are interconnected. The one core issue that led to my downfall in each of these areas of my life was the relationship I had with myself. You see, at some point I had stopped knowing and loving Nicole in the capacity that I needed. I thought I had to do what others wanted me to do and I forgot what I wanted.

Self-love is not selfish—it is necessary. Without self-love, your health, children, family, intimate relationships, occupation, and finances will all suffer. Our mindset toward ourselves and what we can accomplish are huge determining factors in what we are willing to go after. If you feel unworthy, you won't go after anything. Everyone has the capacity to heal their own lives, and that power starts by acknowledging that healing and restoration is needed. The more you think on what you want your life to be, the more action steps you will take to create that life.

You can leave your job, parents, spouse, and even your children, but you can never leave yourself. Take the time to nurture the most important relationship you can ever have. I promise you, you're worth it! We as women try so hard to be perfect. We strive to be the best mother, daughter, sister, friend, wife, and so much more. Striving for excellence is wonderful, but it can become overwhelming. You must take the time to look inward at your individual needs and be sure to take care of yourself. You should be your own biggest fan, not in a sense of vanity, arrogance, or conceit, but in a manner that encourages you to really like and love yourself even with your imperfections. Be fine with your age, weight, height, and personality to the point that you embrace and accept yourself, flaws included. At the end of the day, no matter how hard you try, all you can ever truly be is yourself.

Don't change for anyone other than yourself, because eventually the real you will surface. You don't want to look in the mirror only to see a stranger staring back because you have changed so much for someone else. When you do that, you resent the person for whom you made the changes. Furthermore, if the relationship doesn't work, it can be a long, hard journey to find the real you again. Loving yourself unconditionally means to treat yourself well and to require those around you to do the same. Does this mean that you can force a person to treat you a certain way? No, of course not. You get to choose to leave any situation in which you do not receive the love that you need and desire. Have a healthy dose of respect for yourself and your beliefs, and demand anyone who wants to be around you to treat you just as well.

When it comes to selecting your circle, you must decide if you really want to take a person on their terms or if you want to surround yourself with people in alignment with your terms. Your choices today will shape your tomorrow. To make good choices, you must be willing to learn who you are and what it is you really want. You must believe in yourself enough to only accept people who will enhance your life and be okay with you reaching your goals. You see, it all starts with the mindset of self-love.

The changes I made in myself ultimately led to my overall happiness. Prior to truly loving myself, I believed that I had to take whatever treatment a man would give me; any crumbs of attention were good enough so long as he stayed. I felt as though I had to stay in jobs that were unsatisfying and that my only options were to work for someone else to build their dreams. My children were becoming strangers who lived in the same house, growing up alone while I worked. My finances were a mess, my credit score was ugly, and I wondered if there was ever going to be any hope. I had been trying to handle everything myself. Once I took the time to really see that I needed to step outside and look at my situation from a different perspective, everything became clear.

My self-esteem is on the rise. I am becoming more confident in myself and my abilities to do anything that I set my mind to. I feel healthy and excited about the direction my life is headed. I realize that I do not have to stay in a job where I am doomed any more than I should stay in an unhappy relationship. I have a choice—we all do! You may go through hard times and sacrifice at one point or another, but think of how much it will be worth it to be able to do what you love. I have overcome those obstacles by faith, and this BOSS MOM is preparing to overcome anything else that stands in the way of her dreams. I'm going for mine!

Creative Freedom Boss

AFFTON COLEMAN

Creative freedom has allowed me to be me. I started my journey in life thinking I was supposed to be in financial industry because, growing up, that was what I saw at home. As I got older, I realized that I can be in charge of my own destiny by doing things my own way.

I never knew that I would end up where I am now. My life has had its share of ups and downs and I have always done what I can to make the best of any situation. I always envisioned myself being a successful person but there were so many things that I thought I was good at and I couldn't decide on one thing that would suit my life.

In high school, I was a thriving student in various academic programs. I tried being a star athlete, but I realized that would not be a part of my life because I did not actually master the craft of sports. So, I stayed in my academic lane throughout the rest of my high school years. While on this track, I felt like something was missing in my life and I did not know what it exactly was. What I can say is that, during that part of my life, I ended up doing a lot of things that were out of my character in the hopes of fitting in—I did not want to be labeled as a nerd, a person without friends or boyfriends. While trying to make it, I ended up getting pregnant in the tenth grade. I learned about all my options regarding this pregnancy and quickly learned the ramifications of my actions. I had no choice but to take full responsibility for what was about to become my new life.

This life was exactly what I thought it would be: new! By the time my son was born, I was a junior in high school and I had to learn how to juggle academics with a new kid. I did have some family support but they told me that my son was my responsibility and I totally agreed. Knowing that I would have to make it on my own for myself and my child, the wheels truly started turning in my head when it came to making plans for our future. I decided to do my very best in school and obtain as many scholarships as I possibly could while being accepted into colleges of my choice. My plan and goal at the time was to go into accounting because that was the career my mom was in and I thought I wanted the same. But as time went on, I started my entrepreneurial journey early (though I didn't know it at the time). I began tutoring my peers in to help them pass and ace their classes and eventually graduate. I charged them no money since I felt like I was just helping someone out in the way I hoped someone else would do for me.

Acceptance letters were coming in with different awards but schools were reluctant to allow my son to come to live with me. Fortunately, I was accepted into the University of Missouri-Columbia with a full ride scholarship and allowed to bring my son with me to live in a campus apartment as a freshman. But once I moved to Columbia, I was faced with the hard truth that I was truly on my own and it was up to me to make the right decisions for our future. We struggled for the first two years with me being a college student, single parent, and new adult all at the same time. I had some success with school, so I stayed focus on that, believing this was how my life was supposed to flow. But I changed my degree several times because I could not decide what I wanted to be. In the end, I earned my degree in general studies with an emphasis on accounting and consumer and family economics.

I learned how to channel that academic and hardworking energy and to also create a social circle that consisted of people who were doing the same things as me. This gave my life a certain stability and reliability. There was not a lot of income coming in so I had to take odd jobs that were advertised in the student halls, the first of which was a position in which I mailed letters. That did not work out, so I tried another company through which I sold fitness products, but that also did not work. Some other adventures came along and I tried them as well but I was not successful at those either. Still, I did not give up on the dream of success. I just knew that I would have to find something else that would be better suited for me.

As I entered the stages of graduating from college, I had to decide what was going to be the next step for our lives because, at this point, not only did I have my son, but I also had a new-born daughter. I had the feeling that, since I had my bachelor's degree, I would be able to conquer the world and any company would want me. With many decisions still unmade, I knew one thing was for sure: wherever my children and I would end up, we would be okay.

After speaking to and receiving guidance from my family, I decided that I would not yet return home and instead start a new life with my children. This meant I was either going to stay near my college campus or go somewhere else. I figured I did not need to stay in the Midwest anymore because I lived in that area my entire life. The kids and I loved warmer weather and so there were three states in mind: California, Florida, or Texas. In our state-choosing process, I looked at companies whose work would align with my degree and who would provide the necessary income to match the cost of living of its state. Going through this made me realize that reality was much harsher than my expectations. While interviewing, my dreams thinned out as I was told over and over again that I needed more experience. The other factor that seemed to hurt us was these states had higher costs of living than what I was used to.

Still, I stayed patient, finally got a successful interview, and landed a job with Barnett Public School in Houston. With this move and new job, I believe that my life would be good and we were all set. The company asked me to move to the city right after I earned my degree, and fortunately, my families made that happen as a graduation gift to me.

We made it to Houston on a Friday and I was supposed to start work that Monday. But Monday came and there was no job waiting for me when I went to the company office. I was sent home on the spot.

I was devastated and completely out of my sorts. I was in a new city and state with two kids, a twelve-hour drive away from home, and very little money to live on. What was I to do? I did not want to call home, but neither did I want to be homeless.

To me, this was a situation that I had created for myself and I was the one who had to deal with it. I first decided to talk to people who might be able help me find an apartment; I had the feeling that those same people might be able to recommend or suggest jobs for me. I contacted two of my friends who were teachers in large districts in Houston. I let them know that I was in a dire situation and needed help getting back into a stable environment. Both of them led me to Houston Independent School District and Aldine Independent School District. I also found WorkSource, which was helpful in finding employment with jobs but also had opportunities available for self-employment. This unfortunate situation made me consider taking a job from an employer, but also earning a second income from self-employment to hold my children and me over between regular paychecks.

I ended up finding different jobs that did take care of our necessities but they were not what I had moved to Houston for. At first, I found work in the airport, pushing travelers to their gate. One of the benefits of this job was that I was able to get cash on a daily basis in addition to my regular income. With that cash, I bought snack bags and resold them to the local kids in the neighborhood, which helped increase my income to where our family started to have consistency and stability. I knew this was not the life we were supposed to have but I refused to accept it as our end. I continued to search for better jobs, and approximately one year later, I was able to gain employment with a better company, FMA Alliances that allowed me to stop selling snacks.

Having one income and one job seemed to be a good life as long as my children were taken care of. But something in me still was not satisfied. I progressed at my job and was even able to earn extra commission checks, in addition to my regular income, as long as I met the company's guidelines. In a way, I felt like I was in control but the company, in the end, still had all the control because they determined what portion of the extra money I would receive. This extra check I received would, at times, be more than one month of my regular pay. So, I started going to work with a goal in mind to earn those extra checks instead of banking on my regular income. This way of life worked for us for four years, but by that time, I was working all the time and missing out on my children's growth. I had to find a way to obtain work-life balance so that I could keep sustaining our family and also be a part of my children's everyday lives.

Once again, I stopped seeking out those extra checks and decided to go into the field of education. I constantly second-guessed my decision because I did not see how I could make a significant additional income as an educator. Besides, I didn't think that students would listen to me. I didn't feel like I had the skills to be an educator. But soon, I found out that there was a program in Texas that allowed people with degrees to go through an alternative certification. To start this process, I quit my job with FMA Alliance and became a teacher's aide. Making this drastic change caused me to take a pay cut of $25,000 a year. I had no other choice but to make sure that I did everything I could to become a teacher.

At the end of the program, I was certified. When I started teaching, the income for the first eight months was low; but after that, it rose to the normal educator's pay. I felt that I should be happy with this new niche I created. There was no need for anything extra. I needed to learn my new profession and perfect my craft. I stopped all sorts of extra income work for two years and I got used to my profession. But once again, I needed more.

Who needs electricity in their homes? Everyone does. I found out my light company had an incentive plan that allowed its customers to receive free electricity on a monthly basis if they referred fifteen customers and those customers kept the service. In addition to that, the company also gave away trips and different incentives for customers. These things really excited me because that meant I could have free months of electricity while saving on travel. I liked the company so much that I wanted to know how to make money with them. I got in touch with the correct representative and got started.

I really felt like I was in business for myself because I had a reputable company behind me and I had a necessary service for people. I went through all the ups and downs of managing a business such as creating flyers and passing them out, having meetings, and educating myself on electricity. But what I found out was that people actually thought I was crazy for offering them electrical services because I was also teaching in school. When I went to my family and tried to convince them to switch their service, they also thought I was in over my head and told me to stick with what I knew. I was able to get one person to join the team with me and worked our business for approximately one year. But when things didn't pan out, I decided to let all my wild dreams go for good. Certain ways of life only last for a certain amount of time.

Four years later, I was invited to a party at a good friend's house. This party was to showcase Park Lane Jewelry. I fell in love with the products and I wanted to be a part of the team. To help my friend out, I also hosted a party and I was able to make money of my own because my own party was a success. This was a defining moment for me because I realized that I was able to move forward with my own sales pitch to have parties. It was so great having an extra income on a weekly basis and extra jewelry on a monthly basis. When I brought my ideas to my friends and family, they were in total support of my business plan. For this business, I traveled the world, met new people who I would have never met, and got out of my comfort zone to make my business work. I learned that, if I stick with something, I will definitely be successful at it. I did this for about a year.

Again and again, I said I was done with business. But every time I tried a new business venture, I noticed that it lasted longer than the one before it. The main thing that I figured out was that, yes, I wanted to have a residual income, but I needed and wanted it to be with something that I love doing. After finishing this last jewelry business, a coworker approached me about creating a math presentation for a program that I use in my classroom. Since it was based off of something that I had used before, I didn't think that it would be that difficult. Still, I was really hesitant because I had never done any presentations like that before. I was given a month to put everything together, and as time drew closer, I made sure that my presentation was special and meaningful. Knowing how jaded and critical educators can be, I wanted my audience to be excited about my information and actually try to use it in their classrooms.

The big day was here and all eyes were on me. I literally had a PowerPoint ready to go, but all of a sudden, I decided that a presentation like that was boring and I was anything but boring. So, instead, I gave my own elevator pitch and showed a video that explored the program through the students' viewpoints, as well as those of teachers. In addition to this, I showed ways to start the program and find pertinent resource. We ended the presentation with a question-and-answer session.

Afterwards, the audience was asked to evaluate my performance. I was thrilled to find that people thought I did a great job! In fact, my administrators told me that I needed to attend a presenters' academy within our district. This academy would allow me to brand myself to create presentations in my profession on skills and programs that I have mastered. Today, this branding allows me to stay in my profession while making another income to help other professionals become better at their jobs. I know that I can't present all the time to make all the income I need, so I supplement that with teaching, tutoring afterschool, Saturday school, and summer school.

I did not realize that what I did as an educator would actually be the same resource I would used to have my second income. I have fallen in love with the education field and feel that I am truly blessed to master my craft. I learned a lot along the way with all of my other adventures because those experiences allowed me to see what parts were not for me and what parts were. Success is in the eye of the beholder. I'm glad that I never gave up on my dreams because, if I would have stopped trying, I would have never known how successful I can be in giving information to those who need it!

Epilogue

I pray this book has made a difference in your life and inspired you to live your dreams unapologetically. If so, share your greatest ah-ha! moments on your Amazon review and comments of your favorite BossMom coauthors' website. Then, invite a friend to grab her own copy so that you can do as my Khaos Boss says and "grow together!"

About the Authors

Deletra Hudson

 Deletra Hudson also known as "The Financial Educator" is the owner of Deletra Hudson, LLC, a financial coaching and consulting firm in St. Louis, Missouri. She has a master's in business administration (MBA) in finance, and is a certified accredited financial analyst (AFA) and master financial planner (MFP) with over twenty years of financial experience with corporations, municipalities, nonprofit agencies, small businesses, churches, and professionals.

Hudson is also the founder of the Financial Wellness Institute of America, a nonprofit organization created to increase financial knowledge for small businesses, professionals, and youth through courses, books, educational systems, and workshops. In 2016, she published her debut children's book, Money Doesn't Grow on Trees, which became the 2017 Smart Money Week's Book of the Year. In 2017, she published her second children's book, *AJ Discovers the $2 Bill*, under her new publishing company, Money Matter$ Publishing.

Hudson is also a wife and a mother of three children.

Connect with Deletra Hudson LLC at www.deletra-hudson.com and on social media platforms under the handle, Deletra Hudson. If you are interested in improving your financial position, visit Financial Wellness Institute of America to get information on membership opportunities.

Brandy Butler

After spending fifteen years as an IT engineer working at major Fortune 500 companies, Brandy Butler left her cushy career to pursue her passions. Today, she helps women entrepreneurs, executives, and companies to create influential brands that attract a steady stream of clients, media, and speaking opportunities.

Butler is a professional speaker, published author, and marketing strategist. Her book, *Girl Just Quit*, has helped thousands of women consider smart job exit strategies. She has been featured in Black Enterprise, Success.com. Huffington Post, Blogging While Brown, BlogHer, The Black Life Coaches Summit, and Podcast Movement. She encourages women to own their worth, create strong senses of well-being, and impact the world in positive ways.

Connect with her on social media platforms via
@iambrandybutler

About the Authors

Arriel Bivens-Biggs

 Arriel Bivens-Biggs is parent engagement specialist who uses the tools of entrepreneurship to reach the masses and help families see that business ownership is an option. As the momager of Mikey, "The Kid Who Knows the Biz," Biggs teaches financial education and literacy to youth, focusing on the tenets of effective communication, personal responsibilities, problem-solving skills, self-esteem, community leadership, and strong relationships.

Biggs is the founder of Young Biz Kidz, a 501c3 non-profit organization that offers positive, diverse, and creative ways to teach economics to younger generations. She also educates, empowers, and equips parents with the self-confidence to support their own Biz Kid. Biggs lives in St. Louis, Missouri with her husband, James Biggs, and their two children, Mikey and Ariel.

To connect, visit her website at
ArrielBiggs.com

Kimberly D.L. Pittman

 Kimberly D. L. Pittman is a certified Christian life coach who specializes in relationships and date-coaching. Her target audience is divorcees who strive to leap into the next chapter of their lives. She chose this particular niche based on experiences within her own personal life, as well as the experiences of those around her.

Prior to turning her focus solely on coaching, Pittman successfully owned and operated KDLP Enterprises, a business and training consulting firm that supported local entrepreneurs in the Duval County area. She is also the author of Calm Sparkle, a fiction novel.

To connect, visit her website
at www.KDLPenterprises.com
and www.CoachKim.net

Candice Cox

 Candice E. Cox is an author, licensed clinical social worker (LCSW), therapist, public speaker, trainer, and KHAOS Koach! Since 2008, she has provided licensed counseling and consulting services to children and families in various settings. In 2014, she started her non-profit, KHAOS (Keep Healing And Overcoming Struggles) Inc. and began implementing trauma-informed programs in schools and community centers to address the lack of social and emotional coping skills taught in home and educational environments. Cox utilizes innovative and experiential treatment modalities to change the focus from being labeled to living life beyond labels.

For more information visit
www.khaosinc.org

Keya McClain

 Keya McClain is the founder and CEO of Empower2Be, a nonprofit organization created to end negative stereotypes associated with women relationships, create networking opportunities, and empower women to pursue their purpose. She worked in the legal field as a legal assistant for fifteen years, serving several years as an assistant case manager to the United States District Court. Today, she is as a life coach, motivational speaker, author of My Words Healed My Soul, and instructor of online paralegal courses.

McClain received her associates in applied science for paralegal studies and paralegal certificate from St. Louis Community College, as well as her bachelor of arts in legal studies and master of arts in legal analysis from Webster University. She is a native of St. Louis, Missouri.

Learn more at
http://keyascoaching.com

Tonita Smith

Tonita Smith is best known for her powerful, transparent book, *The Power of Shut-up Grace*, in which she shares how she learned to gain control over her words and sharp tongue. She is also the founder and chief executive officer of The Purpose Driven Woman, LLC, through which she mentors and teaches women how to identify their purpose through self-improvement and self-awareness mentoring sessions. Her annual sold-out event, Real Women Talk Workshop, helps married and single women develop and maintain healthy relationships.

Smith is a wife, mother of three adult sons, and grandmother of four. She is recognized as a clinical scholar for the Robert Wood Johnson Foundation where she volunteers her time mentoring youth through a violence awareness and prevention program.

Connect with Smith at www.authortonitasmith.com or email her at tonita@authortonitasmith.com

Luberta Lytle

Luberta Lytle is a Christian certified life coach and the owner and proprietor of LL Life Coaching Company. She serves as founding member and mentor for Sisters Influencing Sisters (SIS), a nonprofit organization helping girls grades 5 through 12 navigate their teenage years. Prior to publishing her book *Heal the Hurt*, Lytle contributed a chapter in the Jabez Readers' Choice award-winning book, *Millionaire M.O.M.: Living Dreams, Transforming Lives, and Defying the Odds of Teen Motherhood*, and co-wrote *The She-Preneur Journey*.

Lytle earned her MBA from Lindenwood University, bachelor of science in organizational leadership from Greenville College, and practical nursing certification from Kaskaskia College. She has worked for the Illinois State Government for twenty-nine years and is currently a mental health administrator assisting those with developmental disabilities to obtain life skills training.

A mother of three and grandmother of eleven, Lytle lives in Centralia, Illinois with her husband, Delmore.

To learn more, visit her website at
www.lubertalytle.com

About the Authors

Nicole Harrell-Kelly

 Nicole Harrell-Kelly is the author of Men Don't Always Lie, Sometimes Women Don't Listen, a relationship guide that discusses relationship truths and how to break free and heal from toxic relationships.

Harrell-Kelly is from St. Louis, Missouri. In her spare time, she enjoys attending live music events, watching comedy acts, painting, and spending time with her family and friends.

Contact Harrell-Kelly at
NicoleHarrell.Kelly@gmail.com

Affton Coleman

Affton Coleman is from E. St. Louis, Illinois. After earning her bachelor's degree at the University of Missouri-Columbia, she moved to Texas and worked for the financial field for four years before turning her sights to education.

Coleman has now been an educator for ten years, the last six with the Aldine Independent School District. She has been recognized as the top twenty-five math teachers in the district for her grade level in the district, participated as a member of the Innovate Academy, and presented teaching techniques at the Houston Rti Regional Conference.

Connect with Affton Coleman via email at
afftoncoleman1@gmail.com.

CREATING DISTINCTIVE BOOKS
WITH INTENTIONAL RESULTS

We're a collaborative group of creative masterminds
with a mission to produce high-quality books to position
you for monumental success in the marketplace.

Our professional team of writers, editors, designers,
and marketing strategists work closely together to ensure
that every detail of your book is a clear representation
of the message in your writing.

Want to know more?
Write to us at info@publishyourgift.com
or call (888) 949-6228

Discover great books, exclusive offers, and more at
www.PublishYourGift.com

Connect with us on social media

@publishyourgift

CPSIA information can be obtained
at www.ICGtesting.com
Printed in the USA
FFOW03n1055090418
46210051-47501FF